Johnny Risko
The
Cleveland Rubber Man

Johnny Risko
The
Cleveland Rubber Man

Jerry Fitch

Copyright (Jerry Fitch 2016)

The right of Jerry Fitch to be identified as the author of the work has been asserted by him in accordance with the Copyright, Designs and Patents act 1988

1st edition 2016

Published by Tora Book Publishing

ISBN 978-0-9543924-8-2

All rights reserved. No part of this publication may be reproduced, stored in a retrieval system, or transmitted in any form or by any means, without prior written permission of the publisher, nor be otherwise circulated in any form of cover or binding other than that in which it is published and without a similar condition being imposed on the subsequent purchaser.

While the author has made every reasonable effort to trace the copyright owners for any or all of the photographs in this book, there may be some omissions of credits, for which I apologize. Any amendments, additions or corrections can be forwarded to the publisher.

Layout and Cover Design by Harry Otty © 2016

Dedication

I cannot say enough good things about Bill Chase of Cleveland.

Bill started calling me in 1980, asking boxing questions. As the years have gone by he has proven to be more than an inquiring mind but rather a wonderful friend. His tireless efforts to locate old stories and newspaper articles on Johnny Risko were invaluable and this book never would have happened without his help.

I dedicate this book to Bill and will always be grateful to him.

CONTENTS

Acknowledgements

Introduction
i

"There's a Fat Kid in My Neighborhood"
1

Johnny Fails Big Tests
7

First Big-time Victories
17

Road Warrior
30

Big Victories
36

Winning and Losing
57

Max Schmeling
63

Post Schmeling 1929-30
71

Contending Again 1931-32
82

The Last Hurrah 1933-34
106

The Final Fights 1935-40
125

Retirement
149

Appendix

Record
170

Acknowledgements

The late Dan Taylor's history of Cleveland boxing in the Cleveland Press in 1952, was a wonderful source of information, not only for this effort but previous ones. I would be remiss if I didn't mention our next door neighbor, Dorothy Lloyd. Once upon a time she was married into the Risko family and she supplied me with some very special tidbits about Johnny and his family. I also would like to thank Patrice Hamiter and Nicholas Durda of the Cleveland Public Library (Photograph Collection). As always I owe Harry Otty of Liverpool, England, late of Auckland, New Zealand, a huge thank you for getting this book put together and published. He is a special friend. Thank you, again, to Jim Amato for helping with photos. My son Tad, although not a boxing writer, inspires me greatly with his writing efforts on the Titanic and Maritime History. His ability to write while having a full time job, continuing his education and his busy married life in general, well, it makes me realize with me being retired I have no excuses finding the time to get a book written. Last but not least I give praise to my love Lynda Bibler. Once again she provided me with the guidance and proofreading that I needed and it would be hard to imagine completing any of my books without her help.

Introduction

In 1952 Dan Taylor, one of the more famous writers and historians from Cleveland's "Golden Era" of boxing, wrote a series of articles covering Cleveland's boxing history from the beginning in the late 1880's up until the time Joey Maxim reigned as World Light-heavyweight Champion in 1950-1952. This history of Cleveland boxing by Taylor appeared in The Cleveland Press beginning on January 28, 1952, and ending 106 chapters later. It was very comprehensive. In it Dan Taylor, who not only wrote about boxing but sometimes was involved in promoting it, concluded that up until 1952, when he wrote his series there were really only three major eras of boxing in Cleveland's boxing history. The first was the Johnny Kilbane era, then the Johnny Risko era and last the Jimmy Bivins era. Around the time Johnny Kilbane's career was ending in 1923, Johnny Risko's was beginning. When Risko's career was finishing up in 1939-40, Jimmy Bivins' career was beginning.

As I write this in 2015 my opinion is that this assessment by Dan Taylor of the three major eras in Cleveland boxing history has not changed at all during all these years.

Johnny Risko was indeed a major force in Cleveland boxing. I think anyone who knows the history of Cleveland boxing would not dispute that. But while Johnny Kilbane was a world champion and held the title for more than eleven years and Jimmy Bivins would be in the world ratings for most of his fifteen year professional career, Johnny Risko was more of an enigma. One definition of the word enigma describes it as "Something that baffles understanding and cannot be explained." Another version simply says "Anything difficult to understand; a mystery." I feel those definitions pretty much describe Cleveland's Johnny Risko. He won some amazing fights he probably wasn't expected to win. He also lost quite a few fights to fighters most experts felt he should have easily defeated. His overall record of 80 wins, 53 losses, and 7 draws surely would not overwhelm most historians. While winning 80 fights is special, 53 losses isn't. Out of all of the fighters I wrote about in my 2002 book, Cleveland's Greatest Fighters of All Time, he had the most losses in his career. This however does not define him as a fighter and a force in Cleveland boxing history.

Johnny Risko was very special as an amateur boxer. He possessed a devastating right hand and won 39 of his 59 amateur fights by knockout. However, early in his professional career he badly damaged his right shoulder. This serious injury completely changed his style of fighting, yet he still managed to campaign from 1924 until 1940. In his career he met 13 world champions in 22 bouts and he defeated seven of them. He had eight total wins against the champions. The list of contenders he defeated is a long one too. After Johnny damaged his shoulder in his eighth pro fight he mainly used his left jab and hook as his major weapons. His former devastating right hand was used mostly as a supplemental weapon.

The average fans during Risko's career were probably mostly blue collar workers. Cleveland during this time was made up of a vast mixture of European immigrants. It was truly a melting pot. Johnny was born in 1902 in what was then the Austrian-Hungarian Empire. Where he was born is part of Slovakia today. His family arrived in America in 1908, when Johnny was only six (*The Encyclopedia of Cleveland History*, Van Tassel and Grabowski). His many fans could relate to his aspirations of the "American dream". Johnny was always one of them and didn't forget his roots. It was hard growing up during those times and it made Johnny tough. So win, lose, or draw the fans came out to watch him do battle. Apparently some local fans expected more than Johnny could sometimes deliver and occasionally newspaper reports mentioned fans cheering his opponent and booing him.

In recent years I have read posts on Facebook and other forms of social media where Johnny Risko is sometimes referred to as a "trial horse". The people who post these type of comments apparently don't consider Johnny Risko a contender or worthy of mention as a force in boxing during his time in the ring. I totally disagree and the facts prove I am correct. Johnny Risko was ranked as high as the number two heavyweight in the world and often was listed in the top ten, even later in his career. I must admit writing the Risko story was a lot more challenging than some of the other subjects I have written about. In the past I usually knew most of the fighters I was writing about. For example in the case of Jimmy Bivins, I knew him for over forty years. I never met Johnny Risko as he had already left this good earth when I was a mere seven years old. And although Johnny was married twice, he had no children and I haven't been able to find any close surviving relatives to ask any questions about his life or career.

This effort is my attempt to set the record straight and enlighten young and old boxing fans alike about this special ring warrior who made Cleveland home and thrilled fight fans for a long time. He had an impact not only in Cleveland but in the national boxing scene. I hope readers will realize after reading this story that Johnny Risko was far more than "a trial horse". And even though I consider him an enigma, he was far more than that.

During Johnny Risko's career he was often referred to as "Cleveland's Baker Boy" or "The Cleveland Rubber Man". Johnny worked at the family bakery on the west side of Cleveland, even during his boxing career, thus the reason he was sometimes called "Baker Boy". The "Rubber Man" moniker came after a New York writer observed him taking punches without any obvious ill-effects, like the punches were bouncing off of him. I think of him as an "enigma" because he defied any logic. He started out his career fighting 10-round fights, not preliminary bouts. His career consisted of many hills and valleys but he never could be counted out. He was written off many times, yet somehow managed to work his way back into the ranks of heavyweight contender. Although never a champion he ruined the heavyweight championship aspirations of many other hopefuls.

Johnny died in 1953, at the age of fifty, certainly way too young. Although I never met Johnny Risko when I first started following boxing there were still some of the "oldtimers" around who knew him. With the easy availability of records and newspaper archives in today's world, I have been able to learn much more about Johnny Risko than I ever knew before. I hope by reading this book readers will have a better understanding about what Johnny Risko truly meant not only to his loyal Cleveland fans but also to the fans and experts in the national boxing scene.

December 2015

Johnny Risko
Heavyweight Contender
(Cleveland Public Library photo)

"There's a Fat Kid in My Neighborhood"

In 1921 there was a temporary ban in Cleveland on both professional and amateur boxing. On January 18th of 1922, Mayor Fred Kohler lifted the ban on amateur boxing. It soon began to flourish in Cleveland. Charley Marotta, "father of amateur boxing in Cleveland", was awarded one of the first permits under the Mayor's administration. Marotta held many fight cards at his gym on East 79th Street. When shows became too big they had to be held at Moose Hall, the Cleveland Athletic Club and at the Eagles Club on E. 55th Street. The CAC's activities included staging the District AAU Championships in 1922. Cleveland produced five champions in the tourney: Manny Robbins, flyweight; Louis Raddy, bantamweight; Morrie Kleinman, lightweight; Johnny Rini, welterweight; and Eddie Chuck, middleweight.

1922 found the great Johnny Kilbane inactive for the first time since World War 1. It was obvious that the end of his career was coming soon. The amateurs grew bigger and bigger and other local simon-pure warriors included: Frankie Van, later a famous referee in California, Phil Goldstein, who started the career of Georgie Pace, Joe Botta, Steve Nugent, Johnny Jallas, Andy Moran, Mike Wallace, Tom Jackson, George Vadis, Al Klein, Al McVeigh, Otto Pietz, Joe Spoukoup, Pat Irish, Joe Tremaine (brother of Carl Tremaine), Steve Slovanko, Frankie Keegan, Dave Forbes, Mike Lucas, Al Fredericks and last, but not least Johnny Risko.

Johnny Risko would eventually bring Cleveland more glory and more publicity than any other fighter after the great career of Johnny Kilbane. He actually was a protege of Frankie Stellmack, an amateur in the stable of Danny Dunn. During 1921-22, Frankie Stellmack kept telling Danny Dunn: "There's a fat kid in my neighborhood who wants to be a fighter," and Dunn kept telling Stellmack: "Fat kids can't be fighters."

Finally one day Dunn looked up from his desk on the second floor of his run down gym at West 38th and Detroit Avenue in Cleveland and saw the beaming face of a 230-pound fat kid who said, "I'm Johnny Rich and I wanna be a fighter. Frankie Stellmack told me I should see you." "You're not the guy Stellmack told me about by the name of Risko, are you?" Dunn asked. Johnny explained he was using the name Rich because that was the name they gave him on his baseball team. Risko also explained that he worked at the family bakery on the west side. With his weight well over two hundred pounds Danny Dunn must have figured Risko was sampling a lot of the products from the bakery. Dunn asked him if he had any equipment, and he didn't so he gave him a pair of trunks and told him to go and get dressed.

Risko was a pathetic figure in those early days and his desire to learn and ability to take a punch were his only recommendations. It is said the other members of Dunn's stable used him as a punching bag and knocked him all over the gym. But Johnny came back every day for more and this impressed Danny Dunn. Finally after several months of this Dunn had whittled Risko's weight down to 185 pounds. He then decided to turn him loose on the amateurs. Johnny was a sensation overnight. His name was magic at every place he fought. He developed a dynamite right hand punch and won most of his fights by knockout. He followed up his right hand bombs with good left hooks to the body. Because he ended most of fights in short order several promoters were after him to fight on their cards and even signed him to meet two men in one night. Risko became a feared fighter. However during one particular fight card, Jerry Sachs, the promoter, decided to ban Risko. Sachs explained;

"Now this tournament is open to all steel workers, pig iron hustlers, plane movers and all the other sturdy young mitt pushers in and among our thriving village...with one exception."

And who,' we queried, 'might that be?'

"Can't you guess?" countered M. Sachs. "Why it's the fellow Risko-Johnny Risko, the knockout king. If I allow that fellow in I might as well call off the tournament.

There isn't a sane amateur heavy in Cleveland who wants to go between the ropes with this kayo king.

He may or may not be as good as they say, but he sure has got 'em scared." —*Cleveland Plain Dealer* (12-7-1922)

During one of those programs where he was scheduled to meet two opponents Johnny found what it felt like to be knocked down himself. Danny Dunn had also branched out as a promoter and on one particular card at Moose Hall he scheduled Johnny to meet two fighters out of Toledo; Carl Murphy, who only weighed 170 lbs, and Nick Carr who was an even 200 lbs. Johnny disposed of Murphy in the first round but his match with Carr had barely started when Johnny got hit with a left hook while partially off balance and he hit the canvas with a thud. It shocked Johnny and got him mad. He was up at the count of four and was stunned to hear the crowd imploring Carr to finish him. The fact the fans were rooting for Carr infuriated Risko and he tore into Carr with both hands, knocked him down, had him bleeding from the nose and mouth. Carr survived the round and as Johnny came back to his corner Dunn tried to calm him down. Johnny didn't listen and gave Carr a beating the rest of the fight but couldn't put him down again.

The Mayor of Cleveland, Fred Kohler, selected Charley Marotta to be the first promoter to stage an amateur show at the brand new Public Hall on February 19, 1923. Johnny Risko was just one of the fighters to fill the bill, although he certainly was the main attraction. Fighters from Pittsburgh, Buffalo, Chicago, Ashtabula and Cleveland were represented on the card.

Risko was scheduled to meet Mike Wallace, a streetcar conductor. The crowd was announced as 11,000 and proved that not only was Johnny Risko a huge draw but that local fans craved for boxing after having it banned for many years by various politicians.

When the Risko-Wallace fight finally started the fans were worked up to a frenzy. In the beginning of the fight it appeared the big build up was not going to be a reality. Johnny planted a left hook on Mike's chin, and he hit the canvas. He got up and ran right into a big right hand and hit the deck again. Whether it was the gameness of Wallace, because he got up after both knockdowns, or something else, suddenly the crowd started pulling for Wallace and booing Risko. This inspired Johnny and he chased Wallace all over the ring but never could catch up to him. Wallace held his ground and scored at long range and when the decision was announced in Wallace's favor the fans gave him a terrific ovation.

Fans, promoters and other fight figures alike tried very hard to influence Mayor Kohler to lift the ban on professional boxing. But the Mayor felt that there was no reason to lift the ban as he was well satisfied with the amateurs. In fact the pro ban stayed in place the rest of Mayor Kohler's administration. This ended on January 1, 1924, when a city manager type of government took over with William R. Hopkins in charge. Shortly after Hopkins took office he appointed Edwin D. Barry, his Safety Director, as Chairman of a new boxing commission. It didn't take long for the ban on professional boxing to be lifted. And it didn't take long for Johnny Risko to turn pro.

Johnny Risko started out in the pros the same way he fought in the amateurs, with a devastating right hand and a very useful left hook to the body. This was going to change soon as in his eighth pro fight, in Lorain, Ohio, Johnny was in with a seasoned professional named Homer Smith. Smith had won a lot of fame because earlier he went the distance with Luis Angel Firpo. Johnny was winning his bout with Smith when in the seventh round, he threw a right-hand punch at Smith's head that went wide of the mark. Smith ducked and Risko pitched half across Smith's shoulder. As he fell across Smith's shoulder Johnny tore his right arm loose from its socket. When he came out for the eighth round his arm hung limp at his side. He fought this way the last four rounds to finish the bout, which was called a draw.

Johnny was seriously hurt and out of action for several months. It would change his career.

Johnny Fails Big Tests

History shows that Johnny Risko's career was one of many ups and downs. His amateur career came so easy for him, he stopped 39 opponents in 59 winning bouts. But the injury he suffered to his right shoulder against Homer Smith early in his professional career, changed a lot of things. Where he had been knocking opponents cold with his lethal right hand, now it was not nearly as big a part of his arsenal. He became mostly a left hooker and it made him a different kind of fighter. It could be said that Johnny would experience a roller coaster ride from that point on during his lengthy career.

Management is a huge part of a young fighters career. Matching a fighter with the right type of opponent can sometimes make or break him. Most managers will keep their fighter away from big punchers or certain styles until they are sure he can fight such an opponent. Sometimes it is just a matter of waiting until their fighter gets the proper seasoning before matching him up with someone that might give him a lot of trouble early in his career. To avoid discouraging their fighter while he is still learning the trade a manager may try and match him only with opponents that seem to have the right style their fighter can handle. It is also a reality that some fighters may never match up with certain types or styles of fighters no matter how much experience they gain. If you want to eventually become a contender you will have to fight anyone who stands in your way.

Johnny Risko's first fight, after laying off for three months to allow his shoulder to heal, was against Joe Downey of Columbus, Ohio. That fight took place on September 9, 1924, in Canton, Ohio, and although Johnny only used his left hand for most of the fight, he won easily and stopped Downey in the sixth round.

Apparently that performance impressed Danny Dunn enough that he decided his "Big Fella" as he liked to call him, was ready for much better opposition than Joe Downey offered. So he matched him with lanky Martin Burke of New Orleans, Louisiana, a heavyweight who had been in with some really good fighters. Burke had fought the likes of Fred Fulton, Billy Miske, Tommy Loughran and Chuck Wiggins. He had also gone the distance with Harry Greb once and Gene Tunney twice! Burke and Johnny met on October 1, 1924.

Johnny gave Burke a spirited fight and never showed quit. After the third round it was all Burke, and he gave Risko a boxing lesson. Burke, although never seriously hurting Johnny, landed ten blows to one in many rounds. It was not an exciting fight but there was no doubt who was winning the match after the third round. Burke was the type of fighter that would have given Johnny fits, even on his best night. For a young fighter like Risko this was not a match to build his confidence.

Throughout the rest of 1924 and into 1925, Johnny stayed active. But he wasn't winning important fights against some fighters who he really needed to defeat to make himself relevant in the heavyweight rankings. In fact he lost his first seven big-time fights covering the first year and a half of his professional career. Besides losing to Martin Burke he was beaten by Quentin Romero Rojas, Sully Montgomery, Jack Renault, Young Stribling, Jack Sharkey and eventually Gene Tunney.

The Quentin Romero Rojas fight on November 28, 1924, in Cleveland, was considered at the time to be one of the greatest heavyweight fights in the city's history. Risko showed he could stand up to the sledgehammer blows of a 200-pound fighter without flinching. Risko gave an incredibly brave exhibition according to Dan Taylor. Risko was leading after six rounds but Rojas then took the play away. Johnny rallied to take the last three rounds, and he was unlucky to have referee Billy Sulzman raise Rojas's hand after twelve rounds.

Risko's fight with Jack Sharkey on September 17, 1925, in Boston, was won by the New Englander, according to those who scored the fight, giving him six out of ten rounds. At times it appeared Sharkey was scoring at will during some of the rounds. It was not an easy fight to score. Risko started off the fight with terrific body blows but then Sharkey's left jab started to land more and more. If Risko was lacking, it was not for his effort. Even in victory many locals thought Sharkey's effort was disappointing. Some even felt the fight was a lot closer than the scoring. Risko never stopped trying and was always working his way inside with a body attack, even at the end.

Regarding the November 18, 1925 fight with Gene Tunney, Danny Dunn always maintained that his "Big Fella" gave Tunney a tough time. Like a lot of boxing managers over the years Dunn always said "We did this" when Risko won and "he did that" when Risko lost. Dunn said after their bout Tunney never wanted any part of Johnny again. Once again that is probably a manager talking. When you think of the men Gene Tunney met in his career, not the least Jack Dempsey and Harry Greb, surely there were other reasons why Tunney and Risko never met again. Still I imagine the effort given by Johnny Risko in their bout gave Gene Tunney reason to pause when considering a return match. He had nothing to gain by it.

However the pre-fight predictions by some experts saying Johnny Risko wouldn't last one round were way off.

GENE TUNNEY DUE TO GET IN TODAY.

"He'll Knock Risko Cuckoo," Manager Gibson Wires Ahead.
—*Cleveland Plain Dealer* (11-16-1925)

But the day after the match the headline of the post- fight story by sportswriter, James Doyle told it all:

"Tunney Awarded Decision Over Risko in Classy Fought 12-Round Bout."—*Cleveland Plain Dealer* (11-19-1925)

The *Cleveland Plain Dealer* round by round recap of the fight on November 19, 1925, read exactly as follows:

"Fight By Rounds

ROUND 1 - Risko rushed in and tapped Tunney's ribs then sent a solid right to his opponents stomach. Risko rushed again and rushed Tunney to a corner. Tunney's first blow was a right to the jaw. Risko came back with a left to the body. Risko put his left over again to the body and sent a left to the jaw. They clinched and Risko landed a right to the jaw. On Risko's next rush Tunney met him coming in with a short right to the body. John was wild with a right but scored with a left to the jaw and the crowd applauded as Risko rushed Tunney to retreat. Risko was wild with a left as they clinched.

ROUND 2 - Risko rushed and they clinched, John missing with a left to the head. In another clinch Risko peppered Tunney's jaw. Tunney crossed with a hard right to jaw and repeated. It was the best blow of the fight. It partly staggered Risko. Risko returned to battle but was met with a hard straight right cross. They clinched. Tunney put over rights and lefts to the body, but was a bit wild with a left to the jaw. They clinched. Risko landed a left to the body, but took two neat rights to the jaw. As Tunney missed with another right to the jaw Risko delivered a left to the body. Risko jabbed Tunney with his left as the bell rang.

ROUND 3 - Risko rushed and sent Tunney against the ropes with lefts and rights to the body. Gene, peered a bit, and put over a hard right and repeated. Again Tunney's right found a mark on Risko's jaw and they clinched. After breaking they clinched twice again. Tunney landed a left hook to the chin and they swapped openly. Tunney put over another good left but Risko came back with a left to the body. It was his best blow of the fight. Risko drove Tunney back with a left to the jaw. They clinched. Tunney landed lightly with a left to the jaw. Tunney scored a left jab to the nose at the bell.

ROUND 4 - Risko renewed his attack and forced Tunney against the ropes with lefts and rights to the body. Gene broke the force of these blows with his elbows and peppered Risko with a left. Tunney landed a left to the jaw and took a left in return which appeared to stagger him. As John rushed again Gene met him with a hard left to the body but was driven back by a hard left to the body. Risko put over a stiff left to the body and received a left to the jaw. Tunney hopped in with two hard rights to the body and they clinched. Tunney's hard left found Risko's forehead. Gene tapped with his right and they were sparring at the bell.

ROUND 5 - Tunney landed a right and two lefts to the jaw. He jabbed with his left and repeated and almost sent Risko to his knees with a hard right to the jaw. Fighting at close quarters Tunney scored five or six times with hard rights and Risko seemed to be in trouble. Risko took a left tap the stomach and another left to the jaw. Tunney is now forcing the fight. Fighting at close quarters Tunney put over rights and lefts to the body. Once more Tunney shot that right to the jaw and followed with another left and right to the body. Risko surprised Gene by coming back strongly but was met with more than he offered. Risko jabbed with his left to the jaw and took Tunney's right once more to the face.

ROUND 6 - Risko rushed and they clinched. They repeated the process. Tunney left jabbed twice to Johnny's chin. Risko advancing again was met with a left to the body and a sharp right to the body. Gene put a left to the face and they clinched. A right cross to the jaw rocked Risko. They clinched. Tunney left jabbed to the jaw and pummeled ribs in another clinch. Risko covered up as Tunney aimed rights and lefts to the jaw, then Tunney switched his tactics, swinging rights and lefts to the body. He landed a light left to the jaw at the bell. The action had slowed up in this chapter.

ROUND 7 - Risko advanced and knocked Tunney against the ropes but he smiled and showed that he was not hurt. Tunney retreated. Risko landed a left to the jaw and took a hard right to the jaw in return. Risko jabbed to the stomach and took a hard right jab. Risko then slowed up. Tunney then landed with a left on Risko's face and Johnny showed that he had been hurt. A hard right drove Johnny back to the ropes. As he came out Tunney put over two left jabs to the jaw. Tunney registered with a powerful left to the body as the round ended.

ROUND 8 - Risko was wild with a left and they clinched. John covered up as Gene took the aggressive. Tunney put over a right and left to the jaw and sent rights and lefts to the body as John rushed in. Tunney again scored with rights and lefts to the jaw. Risko charged with a left but received much damage with rights and lefts to the body. Risko's left landed on Tunney's arm but the crowd cheered as if John had injured his opponents kidneys. Risko's rushes were being met with stiff counter attacks. Risko sent over a hard left hook to the jaw and put over another but not as spectacular. They were swapping evenly at the bell.

ROUND 9 - They rushed into a clinch. Risko scored with a left hook the body. As he landed another left hook, he received a right to the jaw. They clinched. As they came out of the clinch Risko's left reached Tunney's jaw, then John Risko connected with a nice right to the stomach and followed with a left to the jaw. Tunney jabbed with a left to the jaw and then hooked with a left to the chin. Tunney's left raised Risko's head. They clinched. Risko's next charge was met with stiff right and left jabs but he kept boring in and landed a good left to the stomach.

ROUND 10 - They tore into clinch. Tunney shot a hard right to the jaw but Risko retaliated with lefts and rights to the body. Tunney jabbed a left to the chin and followed with a stiff right to the jaw. Risko jabbed Tunney with a left hook. Tunney tapped lightly with his left, but his jaw was in the way of a long swing by Risko. They clinched again. Tunney put over a right to the jaw as Risko rushed in. Coming out of some action at close quarters Gene just ducked out of the way of a whistling haymaker. Risko jabbed three times to the jaw without a return and landed a left to the body. They clinched. John was covering up at the bell and Tunney's attack at this point was of no avail.

ROUND 11- Tunney scored two hard rights to Risko's jaw. Then Gene sent a light right to the same spot. Two more lefts of a stiffer variety drove Risko back. They were mixing with Tunney stepping out ahead once more. Another brought blood to Risko's nose. In another attack John was in the way of lefts and rights to the stomach. In an exchange hit John twice to his once. Risko was now in his corner protecting himself as best as he could. Tunney was driving Risko around the ring with left and rights to the body and Risko was in sore distress. Coming out a clinch Risko put a left hook to the head at the bell.

ROUND 12 - Risko swung his left to the head. Tunney put rights and lefts to the stomach. Risko jabbed with a left to the body. Risko ran into a left hook. John was wild with a left intended for Tunney's jaw. Tunney pummelled Risko's midriff. Risko sent another wild left haymaker. Tunney once more made a tattoo on the Cleveland boys stomach. Tunney put over a straight left to Risko's jaw. Risko came back and drove Tunney back with lefts and rights to the jaw. Tunney delivered a light left to the jaw and repeated. They were breaking from a clinch at the bell. Tunney received referee Matt Hinkel's decision."

Johnny Risko (above left) with 'The Fighting Marine', Gene Tunney.

Risko Beats Fitz. Jr. and Berlenbach for First Big-time Victories

Risko was matched with Bob Fitzsimmons Jr., son of the legendary heavyweight, light-heavyweight and middleweight champion, Ruby Bob Fitzsimmons. Although certainly not the great fighter his father was, never the less he was highly regarded at the time. The bout, held the 4th of January in 1926, had Fitzsimmons listed as the favorite based on the fact he had knocked out Quintin Romero Rojas who had defeated Risko. He also lost a very close decision to Young Stribling, who previously defeated Johnny without much trouble.

The fight was fairly even for the first six rounds, but Risko started to make his move in the seventh round. He lost the eighth but won the last four rounds to take the verdict. He even had Fitzsimmons hurt badly in the ninth and in the final round. It was called his best win to date. On January 5, 1926 the report in the *Cleveland Plain Dealer* appeared as follows:

"Fight by Rounds

ROUND 1- They sparred in the center of the ring. Then Risko rushed in with a light left to the body and they clinched. Risko advanced several times but Fitz would tie him up on each occasion. Finally Johnny succeeded in putting over two or three fairly good smashes to the body. Fitzsimmons appeared in this round to have a very feeble punch. His efforts were mainly directed to tying up the Clevelander.

ROUND 2 - Risko rushed and they clinched in the center of the ring. Referee Hinkel warned Risko when Johnny did not break with the best taste. Soon they were in another clinch with Risko pounding away with right and left to the body. Fitzsimmons trying to retaliate had no steam in the blows. Risko ran into a straight left, the best punch Bob had displayed thus far. Fitzsimmons jabbed with his left and Risko was wild with a right over hand swing. They were wrestling at the bell.

ROUND 3 - Risko shot a right to the body and they clinched. Risko landed a left to the body but there was not much behind it. Fitz fought back with lefts and rights to the body. Both swung wildly in a clinch. They clinched again and again. Fitz's left found the mark on Risko's ear, but it was like a love tap. They grappled around the ring and the crowd voiced it's impatience. The bell found them in a clinch.

ROUND 4 - Fitz jabbed with his left, but took a harder left and right to the body in return. Fitz jabbed twice with his left. They clinched. Risko sent a left to the stomach, then another clinch. At close quarters Johnny popped a stiff right to the stomach and repeated. Fitz's left jab reached Risko's nose twice. Then more wrestling and the bell.

ROUND 5 - Risko waded in with a right and left to the body. Fitzsimmons tried to hold on, but Johnny drove him away with several more punches to the body. Fitz's left found Johnny's stomach twice in succession. They swapped evenly at close quarters. Fitz raised Johnny's head with a sharp right to the chin. Risko came back with a right to the body, but was wild with a left to the jaw. Risko was sent off balance for a second with a left to the body. Risko covered up as Fitz tried to put a left and right to the chin. Risko missed a right to the head at the bell.

ROUND 6 - They rushed into a clinch. Fitzsimmons registered with a light right uppercut. Risko accidentally hit Rob low with a left. Fitz did not complain. Risko shot three neat left crosses in a row to Fitz's jaw. Fitz came back with a fair left to the body. They clinched. Risko drove a right to the body. And another. Referee Hinkel warned Risko for another low punch. Fitz jabbed with his left and Risko was wild with a right. Fitz took a stiff left on the jaw.

ROUND 7- They came out fighting and were even in a trade of rights and lefts to the body and stomach. Fitzsimmons hit Risko low and the crowd booed. After a clinch Risko landed a stiff left to the body. Risko missed a left intended for the jaw and swung himself half way around. Risko popped a straight left to Fitz's chin. There was much clinching. Fitz blocked a hard left as the round ended.

ROUND 8 - They met in a clinch as usual. Then three or four more clinches and the crowd was noisy in disapproval. Risko walked into a pair of left jabs but countered with a right to the body. Another left jab caught Risko on the chin and they clinched.

ROUND 9 - They rushed into a clinch again. Risko jabbed to Fitzsimmon's nose. Fitz jabbed twice to Johnny's jaw. Risko put a glancing right to the jaw and followed with a left to the other jaw. They exchanged jabs, each making the other look rather bad. Risko missed with a right haymaker. Risko slammed a hard right to the hell at the bell. It sounded like the best blow of the battle, but it was too high to be of much account.

ROUND 10 - They met almost head on and clinched. Fitzsimmons jabbed with his left. Risko countered with a mild right to the jaw. Fitz seemed to stagger Johnny momentarily with three rights to the mouth. Risko came back with a pair of lefts to Rob's jaw. They clinched. Fitz jabbed Johnny with two lefts and followed with a light right to the jaw. Risko was wild with a right but connected on another to Fitz's jaw. The last blow coming at the bell was a good one.

ROUND 11 - Risko heaved around the ring in a clinch. Risko sent two hard rights to the head and then sidestepped a right uppercut. Risko shot a stiff left to the jaw and the crowd hollered. Johnny then switched his attack to the body and they clinched. Fitzsimmons put a left and right to the jaw without a return. Another clinch. Risko scored with a straight left to the head. They were wrestling at the bell.

ROUND 12 - Risko's left went over Rob's shoulder. They swapped lefts to the head and then clinched. Risko shook Fitz up a wee bit with a right to the jaw and shook him up still more with another to the same spot. Risko missed a left and in doing so walked into a left to the chin. Risko scored with a right at the bell that shook Fitz again."

Johnny lost a decision to Jack Delaney, future light-heavy champ, in a bout held in New York on February 5, 1926, before 18,000 fans who paid $60,000. The score cards gave Delaney six rounds out of ten, but many felt he did not cover himself in glory. Having much more experience than the younger Risko, Delaney was expected to make Risko crumble before his so called mighty right hand. But although Delaney had more experience and ring generalship he was hard pressed at times. Risko did himself proud and was aggressive and landed some heavy blows during the match. Delaney won a unanimous decision but the crowd obviously was in the underdog Risko's corner all the way. The crowd let out a steady jeer when the decision was announced.

Johnny was scheduled on March 19th for another important fight, also in New York. His opponent was Paul Berlenbach, who three months earlier had won the world light-heavyweight title over Mike McTigue. The fight against Berlenbach was the night that Johnny Risko arrived at the big time. He floored Berlenbach twice and won the decision before a crowd of 12,000 fans in Madison Square Garden. This fight is perhaps the first time fans heard Johnny Risko called by the nickname "Rubber Man". Berlenbach was a terrific puncher but when his best shots bounced off of Risko, one of the New York writers dubbed him "The Rubber Man" from Cleveland, and the moniker stuck. The Associated Press said that Risko was a decisive victor. It was only the second fight that Berlenbach had lost in his career up till then. Without a doubt it derailed the ambitions of Berlenbach to land a heavyweight title fight. The *Cleveland Plain Dealer* (03/20/1926) listed the fight by rounds as follows:

"Risko Victory by Rounds

ROUND 1 - Risko was first to land, a left to the stomach. He landed again, right and left to the body. Berly drove his left to the stomach. Berly landed a light right to the body. Risko was jarred by a right to the jaw. He jabbed left to jaw. Berlenbach was short with a left. They clinched. Risko landed a right to the jaw. Risko missed left to the head. Berlenbach landed a left to chest. Berlenbach went down from a left to the head. He was right up. Risko landed again to jaw. Berlenbach was holding on. Risko drove left to head. He landed four or five to head without a return.

ROUND 2 - Risko went right after Berlenbach and missed a swing to the head. They both missed rights. They clinched. Berlenbach fell into a clinch. Risko grazed nose with left. Risko landed left to jaw. Risko landed another left and right to head. Berlenbach sent right to jaw and left to head. They clinched. Risko missed drive for head. Risko missed left. Berlenbach pounded Risko's kidneys. Risko landed another left to the head. They mixed it in the center of the ring. They clinched. Berlenbach sent left to the stomach. They both swung wildly. Berlenbach sent left to body. Risko was carrying fight to Berlenbach. He landed right to jaw. Berlnbach went down from left to jaw. The bell rang as he got up.

ROUND 3 - They sparred. Risko sent a left to stomach. Berlenbach landed right to body but Risko's blows carried more steam. Risko missed right to head. Berlenbach punched right and left to Risko's body. They exchanged heavy rights and lefts in a furious mixup. Risko landed another left to the jaw. Berlenbach sent right to head and was working for Risko's stomach. Another landed on Berly's jaw. Risko repeated without a return. He drove left to Berlenbach's stomach. Berlenbach landed to face. Risko missed. Risko drove Berlenbach to ropes with left and rights to stomach and then sent left and right to head. Risko seemed to connect at will with blows to head. Risko sent left and right to Berlenbach's head. The bell comes to Berly's aid.

ROUND 4 - Berlenbach landed left to head. They both missed. Risko missed left to head. Risko landed right to head. Berlenbach took the aggressive. He landed left to ribs. Paul's left eye was swollen. Risko landed right to jaw. Risko landed vicious right to jaw and missed a left. Berly landed left to kidneys and right to jaww(sic). Risko sent two lefts to Berlenbach's eye. He drove home one to Berly's stomach. Berly uppercut Risko with left and shot three or four to head without slowing Risko up. Risko came back with the same dose. He landed two rights to Berly's jaw. Berly landed left and right to jaw. Risko missed with right. Berlenbach landed left to jaw. Risko retaliates with same as bell rings.

ROUND 5 - Berlenbach landed left to jaw. Risko's left went to head. They mixed it in center of the ring. Risko sent another wild left to head. He caught Berlenbach in the mid section with left. Berlenbach sent left to head and at close quarters landed with left to ribs. Risko missed with left. Berly landed three or four to Risko's jaw without slowing him up. Risko sent right to jaw. Berlenbach ducked under a right and sent left and right to stomach. They mixed it in the middle of the ring. Risko sent hard right to jaw. He landed a second and followed with a left. Risko missed with right but landed left to head. Risko sent Berlenbach against the ropes with a right to stomach.

ROUND 6 - Berly sent right and left to jaw. Risko sent left to head and they clinched. Risko sent left to head and missed with a right. Berlenbach landed a right to ribs and they clinched. Risko sent left to head and received a right in return. Berly punished Risko against ropes and John went after Berly in a neutral corner. Berly sent left to Risko's head and right to nose which shook John. Risko sent right to head. Berlenbach landed twice to head. Risko missed wild right and almost fell. They clinched. Berlenbach at close quarters worked his right to face. Risko missed left to head and Berlenbach sent left to face. Risko landed hard right to jaw. Berly came right back with the same thing.

ROUND 7- Risko missed left. He landed a left to ribs. Berly sent right and left to stomach. He landed left and right to Risko's face and stomach. Risko missed with left. Risko was missing many blows and Berlenbach landed twice to kidneys. They clinched. Berlenbach blocked a wicked left and sent right to Risko's head, then repeated to the body. Risko landed left to stomach. Berly sent left to stomach. Berly was parrying many of Risko's swings. Risko landed one on Paul's head. They clinched and Berly landed on John's kidneys. Risko landed a heavy right to jaw. Berlenbach didn't seem to solve Risko's guard. At the bell Berly was pounding Risko's ribs and kidneys.

ROUND 8 - They both missed rights. Berlenbach jabbed without effect. Risko pinned Berlenbach's head and sent two rights to jaw. He sent left to Berlenbach's jaw. Berlenbach landed left and right to Risko's chin. They exchanged lefts and rights to head in center of the ring. They clinched. Berlenbach drove three to Risko's chin at close quarters. Berly landed left and two rights to John's face. Berly stopped a left to head. Risko was swinging wildly. They clinched. Berly landed one on John's neck. Berly sent left to jaw. Risko sent left and right to stomach. Risko landed hard right to chin. They clinched.

ROUND 9 - Berlenbach landed right to head. Risko's landed left to head. The string in Berly's tights broke and the fight was halted momentarily. They went into a clinch and both landed with rights and lefts. Risko sent vicious right to Berlenbach's head. He punished Berlenbach severely in neutral corner. Risko was driving rights and lefts to ribs. Risko missed wild left. Berly assumed the offensive. The referee had to fix Berly's tights and Risko walked around with disgusted look. Risko landed on back of Paul's head. Berly sent both hands to mid section. Berly stopped a right to jaw and left to ear. Risko sent hard right to jaw and then both hands to stomach. Berly fell into a clinch at the bell.

ROUND 10 - Berly missed with left. They sparred. Berly landed left and right to body. Risko sent left and right to chin. Berly landed left to head. Risko missed with left. Risko stopped an uppercut and sent his left to stomach. A vicious right glanced over Berly's head. John sent left to head and hard right to stomach. A vicious right glanced over Berly's head. John sent left to head and hard right to stomach. Berlenbach sent several lefts and rights to jaw and received several rights in return. Berlenbach was punishing Risko with both hands in middle of ring. Johnny came back strong and forced Berlenbach to ropes. Risko almost floored Berlenbach with a right. They both swung wildly, hoping for a haymaker. Risko landed with right to head. Berlenbach sent two rights to the head and left to face at the bell."

Johnny kept busy and met his previous conqueror, Quintin Romero Rojas, on April 19th in Buffalo, New York. The day of the fight James E. Doyle (*Cleveland Plain Dealer* April 19, 1926) wrote;

"Cleveland Battler Is Favorite to Win". He went on to say "That 'Rock'em' Youth Has Come Fast, While Quintin Has Receded Since Last Meeting."

Manager Danny Dunn always maintained that his fighter deserved the nod the first time Risko and Rojas met. That was debatable and certainly not the first time Dunn claimed his "Big Fella" had been robbed. In this rematch Johnny left no doubt as he tore into Rojas from the beginning and launched a body attack that floored the Chilean in the third round. In the fourth Risko cut Rojas over his left eye. Although both

men traded leather it appeared Rojas was not willing to fight enough to win. Every time Risko landed a body shot, and he landed many of those, Rojas would try to claim he was fouled. Funny thing though the only one getting warnings for low blows during the bout was Rojas. No doubt at the end who the winner was this time.
Although it was not mentioned during the fight apparently Risko had injured his right hand bouncing it off of Rojas' head.

Johnny was scheduled to meet Young Stribling again, this time in New York. The Georgia battler was on quite a winning streak. Since losing a newspaper decision to Jimmy Delaney on February 27, 1925, he had rung up 32 wins without defeat heading into the Risko fight. Overall he had a stellar record of 52-7-2, with far more experience than Risko did. When they met the first time in July of 1925, in East Chicago, Stribling was awarded a 10-round "Newspaper Decision".

Risko and Stribling were scheduled for Madison Square Garden on May 14, 1926, before a packed house of over 12,000. It was a very important fight for both men. Unfortunately for Johnny he had indeed damaged his right hand during the Rojas fight and was left without a full arsenal. He entered the fight with a badly swollen right hand. To add insult to his injury Stribling didn't want to mix it up with Johnny and mostly stood sideways during the bout offering Risko a small target. He used his long left to keep the Cleveland "Rubber Man" at bay. Meanwhile he piled up points. The eighth round was Johnny's best as he brought his left hook into play and bloodied Stribling's nose. He also landed many body shots in the last couple rounds. But it was

Jerry Fitch

Johnny Risko and the great Young Stribling (above - Cleveland Public Library photo) and both fighters with their wives(below).

too little, too late. At the end of the fight Johnny skipped effortlessly to the corner while Stribling seemed totally spent. However there was no doubt who had won the decision, and it certainly was a setback for Risko.

Johnny was scheduled for his first local fight in six months, when he was set to meet Leo Gates, an Indian from Adams, Mass., at Taylor Bowl on June 16th. Risko lost this fight on a foul in the fifth round. He had sent a sweeping left hook below the belt that perhaps robbed him of his most impressive local victory.

Johnny did not have any local fights for over the next six months so he became a road warrior, fighting in other cities far more often than he ever had before.

Road Warrior

Risko's career continued mostly away from Cleveland, at many venues against a variety of opponents. Most of the time however Johnny was not impressing fans or the people who rated fighters as his up and down career continued. After the Gates fiasco he signed to meet former light-heavyweight champion, Mike McTigue in New York. He lost a 10-round decision. The July 2, 1926 *Cleveland Plain Dealer* headlines read:

"Mike McTigue whips Johnny Risko in New York"

Beneath that heading it read:

"Big Rubber Man is Given Ring Lesson"

The blow by blow ring account clearly told the tale:

"Foxy Veteran Easily Earns Decision Before Small Crowd in Ten-Round Bout"

Less than two weeks later Johnny won a 10-round decision over Emilio Solomon in St. Louis. Then it was on to Boston for a match up with Tommy Loughran on July 30th. This was another major match for Risko in his early career. At the end of the fight Loughran's hand was raised. A few days later however, according to Jack Conway, veteran Boston boxing writer,

"The majority of the spectators who witnessed the recent meeting of Johnny Risko and Tommy Loughran figured Risko's aggressiveness should have gained him the verdict."

Johnny was learning that when you fought away from your hometown in your opponents territory the chances of gaining a close decision was difficult at best. Loughran was from Philadelphia, but often fought in Boston, New York and other places in the east. Loughran was in route to a title match with Mike McTigue for the vacant light-heavy title. They would eventually meet on October 7, 1927, in New York and Tommy Loughran would come out victorious.

On August 11th Risko defeated Leo Gates in ten rounds. Previously he had lost to Gates by a foul. Then he continued on the road and didn't distinguish himself at all. Fighting such men as Harry Persson, Pat McCarty, Bob Lawson, George Manley, Eddie Huffman, George Manley again, and Jimmy Delaney, the best he could do was win one, lose three and be held to a draw in three other bouts throughout the rest of 1926.

1927 did not start out much better. Fighting as a substitute against Chuck Wiggins, in Cleveland, on January 31st, Risko was out of shape after not fighting for almost two months. Wiggins had fought Johnny twice before, winning once by kayo in a bout Risko claimed he was fouled.

The second fight was called a newspaper decision draw by some accounts and a decision win for Risko in others. In their third fight Risko built up a huge lead after seven rounds but ran out of gas. Wiggins won the 10th, 11th and 12th round and dropped Risko to his knees in the final round with a body punch that Risko claimed was a foul. Referee Pat Haley would not allow it however, and the fight resumed. Haley called the fight a draw but most everyone in the crowd of 9,000 thought Risko deserved the nod.

In his next seven fights Johnny Risko continued to puzzle many fight buffs as he didn't win most of the fights he should have. He lost to Tommy Loughran again on February 15th, also dropped a newspaper decision to Chuck Wiggins in Indianapolis on March 14th. Wiggins was certainly never an easy foe for Johnny. Wiggins was not afraid to fight anyone. He actually met the great Harry Greb nine different times in his career.

Johnny lost by a foul to Jimmy Slattery in Buffalo on March 28th. His ring style often found him charging into an opponent and some of his punches sometimes went astray. If an opponent would fight Johnny dirty, he got the full wrath of Johnny in return. Some referees were quick to pick up on this.

It can safely be said, however, that many of Risko's decision losses could be questioned because of the way fights were judged in that era. Fighting in an opponent's hometown almost always guaranteed any newspaper decision would go to the local boy. And Johnny fought in his opponent's backyard more often than not during his lengthy career.

Some newspaper accounts mentioned that Danny Dunn felt Johnny wasn't always in the best of shape for all of his fights. Still his efforts usually were strong, he tried hard, and nobody was stopping him or ever would. Beginning with his April 19th fight in Wilkes-Barre, Pennsylvania, against old foe, Quintin Romero Rojas, Johnny would finally start out on an extended winning streak. He beat Rojas over ten rounds and then fought two or three times a month against almost every type of opponent available during the summer. He won against Jimmy Lester in New York on May 9th, Tiny Jim Herman in Fremont, Ohio, on the 26th, drew with Joe Sekyra in Dayton, Ohio, on June 6th, then defeated Chief Metoquah in Indianapolis on June 22nd. He knocked out Sully Montgomery in the 3rd round in Canton, Ohio, on July 4th and won over Jack DeMave of New York in Cleveland at the Olympic Arena, on July 13th. Risko won nine of 10 rounds and floored DeMave for the count of eight in the seventh round with a dynamite left hook to the jaw.

Johnny continued on with a victory over Lou Scozza in Buffalo, on July 21st, Red Hanlon in Seattle on August 16th and Jack Gagnon in Boston on August 25th. He again defeated Joe Sekyra in Dayton on the 31st and then was scheduled to meet Jack Delaney in Cleveland on September 14th.

Walter Taylor, one of Cleveland's premier promoters during this time frame scheduled Johnny to meet the former light-heavy champ in the closing match of the outdoor season.

The fight was held at The Taylor Bowl, which was an outdoor arena Walter Taylor had built on Harvard Avenue. Although Risko outweighed Delaney by 20 pounds the experts felt that Delaney's superior boxing skills would be too much for the Cleveland "Rubber Man". But Johnny had a big surprise for everyone and instead of lowering his head and charging forward as he often did in many of his matches, he came out boxing. He won the first five rounds easily as he stuck out his jab. He jarred the former champ around the ring, adding an occasional left hook and right hands to the body to keep Jack honest. Delaney hurt Risko twice in the sixth round according to Dan Taylor in his 1952, Cleveland Press series. But Risko recovered and although Delaney closed with a rush, Johnny fought well enough in the late rounds to protect his lead. It was a big win.

Johnny met Quintin Romero Rojas again, this time in Akron on October 13, 1927, and he won the decision. The next bout possibly changed history as far as Risko's ring ambitions were concerned. He was scheduled to meet Tom Heeney, the New Zealander, who was often called "The Hard Rock From Down Under" on October 26th, in Detroit. Heeney at the time of the Risko fight had defeated Phil Scott, won and lost against Paulino Uzcudun, defeated Jack DeMave and knocked out Jimmy Maloney in the first round.

The Risko and Heeney camp had a dispute about who would be the referee for the bout and Risko found himself down 6 to 5 in the betting odds prior to the fight. He had a nine pound weight disadvantage, weighing 187 to Heeney's 196. Still many experts felt Johnny was on a roll and would defeat the New Zealander and continue his climb up the ranks. The fight would not turn out as favorable as Johnny and Danny Dunn had hoped and would be the only blemish on Johnny's winning streak. Johnny lost the decision but it was more than a loss, it was a huge loss. Tom Heeney would fight to a draw with Jack Sharkey after his win over Risko and then defeated Jack Delaney by decision. He was then signed to fight Gene Tunney for the heavyweight title on July 26, 1928. He was stopped via a 11th round TKO. Gene Tunney would retire from the ring after the Heeney defense. It can be debated whether the Heeney loss should or should not have prevented Johnny Risko from missing out on a title shot against Gene Tunney. There are reasons for that theory because after the Heeney loss Johnny would win some of his biggest victories. It became a mute point when Tunney decided to call it quits.

Johnny Risko - Contender

Big Victories

After the Heeney defeat Johnny signed to meet Paulino Uzcudun in New York on November 25th. The Basque was being groomed by Tex Rickard for a title shot against Gene Tunney. He had defeated Harry Wills, Tom Heeney and Knute Hanson, the Swedish giant. Tex Rickard had been looking for an excuse to sidetrack Risko and the Heeney defeat was all he needed. However Johnny didn't stay sidetracked for long. Johnny upset all the dope in this one as he won clearly in ten rounds. He gave Uzcudun a bad beating, coming close to knocking him out in the 10th round. It was considered at the time one of the greatest heavyweight fights in New York history. The Brooklyn Daily News had the following headline in the November 26, 1927 edition:

"Rickard Got The 'Worm of his Eyes Apple' in Uzcudun's Defeat"

In his next contest on December 7th Johnny met Phil Scott of Great Britain in Cleveland. Scott was called "Fainting Phil

Scott" but had been taken over by Billy Gibson, former manager of Benny Leonard. Johnny continued his "Spoiler" role in this bout on Ed Bang's annual News Christmas Toy Shop Fund show. Johnny beat Scott at his own game. Scott, the better puncher was out-punched and floored in the seventh round. The decision was clear in Johnny's favor.

This victory gave Johnny Risko another shot at Jack Sharkey, the future heavyweight champion on March 12th. Newspaper accounts said that the winner of this particular battle would get a shot at Gene Tunney for the title in the summer.

Premier promoter, Tex Rickard was quoted in the Plain Dealer on January 25, 1928, as saying he had no knowledge of such an agreement, as previously quoted in Boston dispatches. Rickard claimed that Tom Heeney and Jack Delaney were still in the running but did not commit himself to Sharkey or Risko. The Sharkey camp even claimed they had a signed contract. Jess MacMahon, Madison Square Garden matchmaker, had stated: "I have spoken with Gene Tunney and he agrees to fight the winner of the Sharkey-Risko encounter." He went on to further say that "Tunney thinks highly of Risko in view of his decisive victories over Delaney and Paulino."

Risko met the future heavyweight champion, Jack Sharkey in New York and defeated him handily over fifteen rounds. It was listed as a split decision but most every writer and expert felt that Johnny had earned the nod easily enough. This fight found Jack Sharkey talking and insulting Risko throughout the fight. He did his usual complaining to the referee about low blows too. Some of the quotes included Sharkey calling Risko a "Bohunk tramp" referring to his heritage and telling him, "You are a big bum" and Risko would say, "Maybe I am a big Bohunk tramp, but you must be bigger one a'reddy, you bum, cuss I am lickin' you from here to hell!"

The following was printed in the *Cleveland Plain Dealer* on March 13th, 1928:

"Fight By Rounds

ROUND 1 - Grimly intent on his business, a different fighter from the man who jogged against Tom Heeney, Sharkey tore from his corner to nail Risko with a right to the body. Johnny got mad and buried his left hook deep into Sharkey's ribs. Sharkey bent double, grunted, and took two smashing left hooks on the chin as he straightened up. Again Risko drummed a heavy left hook to the pit of the Boston gob's body. Jack came in close, lashed both hands to Risko's head, and dropped his right dangerously close to the foul line. Risko, thoroughly aroused, was smashing him heartily about the body at the bell.

ROUND 2 - Risko was taking a lesson from Heeney's book, forcing the fighting and clubbing steadily to Sharkey's body. Johnny nearly dropped Sharkey with a left hook to the chin that sounded all over the house. Two more lefts to the body and another short right to the chin hurt Sharkey badly. He fell into a clinch, clinging tightly as he tried to shake the cob webs from his brain. Risko played his left carefully to the body as Sharkey danced away. Sharkey was wild with a left hand but clubbed two massive rights under Risko's heart just before the bell. The punches sent Johnny to his corner looking a bit pained.

ROUND 3 - Risko met Sharkey's plunging attack with a left slug into the ribs. Jack bounced up and down, stabbing with his left, and ripping a short right to the heart as Risko piled all over him, impervious to punishment. Sharkey's right hand punching to the body slowed the Austrian a bit, and he went on the defensive. Sharkey boxed about him in dazzling fashion, pecking nicely with a left. He dropped a right on Risko's heart that hurt the doughnut maker at the bell.

ROUND 4 - Sharkey met the pudgy Cleveland youth at his own game. They hammered rights and lefts to the heart and ribs for almost half a minute. Sharkey was careful after that and danced away. As Risko followed a left and right crashed full into Johnny's head and nearly toppled him. He swayed a bit on his legs as the Boston gob belted his body in an effort to open the way for a finishing shot. When the opening came Sharkey missed a full right smash to the chin by inches and Risko fell inside, swapping them to the body, safe for the time being, The bell rang as they drummed each other's ribs.

ROUND 5 - Sharkey looked a complete master of the situation as he boxed cleverly away from Risko's leads. But Risko bidding his own strike, suddenly lined a left hook deep in Sharkey's body. They swapped freely at close range and Risko blinked dizzily as rights and lefts suddenly crashed to his chin from all sides. Sharkey met the baker continually with a straight left jab and then crashed his right resoundingly under the heart. Risko was quite mussed and grinning crookedly at the bell.

ROUND 6 - Sharkey made the pudgy Austrian look flat footed and clumsy as he boxed him prettily and twisted him around at will in the clinches. Johnny manfully dove for close quarters, pinned the sailorman on the ropes and hammered both hands to the body. A short hook opened a cut over Sharkey's right eye. The referee warned Risko and the crowd booed disapproval as Johnny sprayed a backhand across the eyes. Sharkey tried to box carefully at long range but Risko stormed in to flail him about the body with choppy hooks. Sharkey was staggering as he kept Risko away by feinting ferociously right up the bell.

ROUND 7 - Sharkey was carefully aggressive. He lost it, however, when Risko suddenly got inside his guard and fired both hands to the body. Jack screwed up his face apparently in pain, and complained to the referee. The arbiter motioned them on, and Risko flashed another left handed volley into the Boston boy's head and body. Sharkey nailed Johnny with a short right uppercut coming in but he could not keep Risko from lathering his ribs with more short hooks. The crowd booed derision as Sharkey held desperately under the storm of the body punishment.

ROUND 8 - Sharkey tore in, left hook following to the body, but Risko hustled him right into a corner for another dose of body battering. The battle was strictly a matter of body bruising and both fired their huskiest shots to the ribs. Sharkey kept both hands across his mid-section as he went back to long range firing. He flung a grueling right under Risko's heart at the gong.

ROUND 9 - Sharkey drilled over a left hook to the chin and Risko promptly went wild. He bowled the Boston boy into the ropes, ripping and tearing at his body with both hands. That looping left hook whacked twice full on Sharkey's chin as they struggled out to the center of the ring. Then Sharkey went to the body, his left and right nestling solidly under Risko's short ribs. Two full body mashes hurt the Westerner, and a right uppercut shook him coming in, but with one full left smash to the chin Risko nearly knocked Sharkey clean from the ring a few seconds before the gong sounded. The smash dizzied Sharkey and did more damage to his injured right eye.

ROUND 10 - Risko flailed into Sharkey at the bell, chased him into a corner, and sunk him for a count of three with a left and right to the body. Sharkey apparently slipped under the blows for he came up unhurt and rapped into Risko with his arms plunging like pistons to the stomach. Three times, as Risko missed right swings, Sharkey buried his left hook full in the pit of the Rubberman's body. Sharkey danced around, plenty of action in his knees, while Risko hung on heavily, stung by the body blows, until the gong.

ROUND 11 - Risko boxed a little, didn't get far, and drove his favorite left hook back into Sharkey's body. For the hundredth time, at least, they fell together and crunched short pokes to the body. As they drew their hands back, blood trickled down from a bad cut over Risko's right eye. Sharkey took heart at the sight and ripped into Risko's stomach with both hands, Risko appeared to be losing steam under Sharkey's relentless and clever attack while the flow of blood from his damaged eye made him blink frequently. Sharkey went to his corner fresh and dancing at the bell.

ROUND 12 - As they fell in close at the opening gong, slashing and poking to the lower region, the battle of Sharkey's short right to the heart appeared to be edging out ahead of Risko's left hook to the pit of the stomach. Jack lashed out a straight left and again hammered his left to his favorite spot. Risko closed in desperately and nailed Sharkey with a left hook that threw the sailor into the ropes. Gaining new momentum, Risko pounded Sharkey's body. They looked each other over for a moment, then fell in close again to slug monotonously at each other's ribs until the gong.

ROUND 13 - The battle was failing absolutely to disclose anything spectacular in the way of a heavyweight contender. Sharkey stabbed and stabbed with his left until Risko walked right into him with a volley of lefts and rights to the head and body that suddenly shook the Boston sailorman. He bounced back into the ropes, came out in a dive, and grabbed Risko tightly. The crowd booed as Sharkey held desperately and Risko vainly punched and hauled to do what little damage he could. Sharkey tired, and Risko flailed him from one rope to another, a left hook crackled on Sharkey's chin. Two rights dug deep in his body and his seconds had the smelling salts all ready when the round ended.

ROUND 14 - Not content with the margin he appeared to have piled up already, Risko ripped wildly into Sharkey's body.

Jack complained bitterly to the referee about low punches that were nicking his ribs. He fell again into Risko's style of fighting, short bruising body slashing at cheek to cheek range, and he was getting steadily the worst of it. Making a stand with his back to the ropes, Sharkey ripped a right uppercut to Risko's chin, but held tightly instead of following up his advantage. Risko was unhurt and he slugged, slammed and tore at Sharkey's body right up the bell.

ROUND 15 - They shook hands for the final round. Risko promptly ripped both hands to the body as though the fight was just starting. Sharkey suddenly found his opening and drove two crashing right handers to Risko's chin. Johnny grunted as Sharkey's right and left hammered under his heart. Risko missed a left hook and nearly floored the referee, Kid McPartland. As Sharkey stabbed with his left, Risko once again dropped in close with both hands drilling to the pit of the stomach. Sharkey held continually in the clinches, but landed another crashing right to the chin just before the final bell."

In the Tuesday, March 13th *Cleveland Plain Dealer*, Light-heavyweight champion, Tommy Loughran wrote a column about the Sharkey-Risko fight.

NEW YORK, March 12, "Just as I predicted, Johnny Risko defeated Jack Sharkey in their fifteen-round fight here tonight. The experience the Cleveland Baker got at the hands of the light heavyweights enabled him to outsmart his faster opponent. Sharkey has always been called a boxer, though I don't know why. In tonight's battle the sailor was all at sea when

Risko would not lead to him. If Sharkey was the boxer he is supposed to be he would have known enough to feint, step back and lead Johnny on. Risko fooled the fans and Sharkey by not fighting his usual tearing in, mauling sort of battle, and by the use of the left jab. This jab raked Sharkey's stomach, bewildering him to the extent of upsetting all his plans. Jack once again showed that his body is weak. This was a fact before he fought Jack Dempsey and it was proven once again."

After the Sharkey fight Danny Dunn kept Johnny busy. Even though Rickard apparently didn't want Risko as a title challenger Dunn and Risko felt the public would decide the matter. So Johnny was signed to meet the giant George Godfrey, in Brooklyn, New York, on June 27th.

Godfrey was a giant of a man compared to Risko, standing 6' 3" tall and weighing in the vicinity of 235 lbs. He was heavy muscled and standing next to Johnny at the weigh-in he looked much larger than that. George had defeated the likes of Martin Burke, Fred Fulton, Larry Gains, Paulino Uzcudun and Jimmy Maloney. He had also met and lost to Jack Sharkey and Primo Carnera. He was a formidable opponent who would go on to score 78 knockouts in his 96 career victories. One of the great quotes happened during the the weigh-in for the Risko-Godfrey bout.

According to sources when Johnny saw the size of Godfrey he said, *"Holy smoke, Dan!"* as the Dark Menace stood on the scales. *"Ain't he a big guy tho!"* Dan obviously felt the same, *"He sure is, John."* said Mr. Dunn. *"Yup,"* said Johnny, *"he's SO big that I don't see how I can miss him."* And the record book tells that the Risk' wasn't wrong on his figuring.

Although the fight itself would end up a lot closer than Danny Dunn, trainer Charley Goldman, or Risko himself would have wanted, Johnny was victorious.

The fight report in *The Charlestown Daily Mail* (28 June 1928) appeared exactly as follows:

"Johnny Risko Spoils Hopes Of George Godfrey For Boxing Fame, Fast Finish Made By Cleveland Pug
Thrilling rally in Last Two Rounds Believed To Have Decided Profit Made in Tilt

One Of The Few Financial Successes Of Summer's Outdoor Ring Season

Once more that pudgy Clevelander, spoiler of heavyweight favorites, doughy Johnny Risko, has battered out of the limelight a man generally picked to defeat him.

This time the victim was George Godfrey, successor to Harry Wills as the current "Black Menace" and the man generally avoided by all heavyweights who seek advancement in their profession. To (sic) Risko was awarded the victory after 10 rounds of vicious, bruising mauling last night in the ball park of the Brooklyn Nationals, Ebbets Field.

Critics Don't Agree

Although the verdict of the judges met with only luke warm approval from the 25,000 fans, several sports writers gave Risko a margin of five rounds with four for Godfrey and one even. The Associated Press score sheet gave the Negro giant five rounds, with three for Risko and two even.

Risko apparently caught the judge's eyes with a thrilling rally in the last two rounds that had the 235-pound Negro giant glad to hold and back away from the stress of left hooks Johnny threw at his head and body. There was no semblance of a knockdown and neither bore marks of the battle at the close.

The warfare for the most part was at close range, with a premium on clouts to the ribs that rarely bothered either battler. Risko absorbed Godfrey's right hand smashes and came back smiling for more while the best shots of the Cleveland boy hardly dented the man mountain opposite him.

Legs Bother

In the early rounds Godfrey toyed with the rushing youngster who spoiled Jack Sharkey, Jack Delaney and others as drawing cards in Tex Rickard's elimination tournament last winter. But the great bulk of his frame wrestled heavily on the Negro's slender legs in the last five rounds and Johnny, plugging steadily forward, left hand wining ahead to take the verdict.

The match was one of the few financial successes of the rainy summer season of many postponements.

Receipts were $51,684.

ROUND - BY - ROUND

Round One
Godfrey, a smiling giant compared to the squat and pugly Risko, hammered a left and right on the Cleveland boy's body. Risko bounced his famous left hook off the Negro's body and shot two overhand rights to the head. Risko steeped rather easily around the slow moving, ponderous giant, landing easily with his left, but there was danger always in the smashing right Godfrey used steadily as a counter.

Round Two
Risko bounced forward into a flood of left hooks to the head, that the Negro growing vicious, smashed accurately to their marks. Under the storm of blows as Godfrey threw everything into the attack, Risko wilted and the giant Negro nearly wrestled him to the floor. Risko held a moment to gain his wind, then flailed into the huge Negro with overhand rights that had Godfrey holding at the bell.

Round Three
Risko tugged and hauled Big George, almost pulling himself from his feet as he tried to cut the huge black down to his own size with body punches. George took to holding and countering with his right as Johnny stormed into him, throwing caution to the winds. Risko, a pigmy besides Godfrey's massive hulk, still had the courage to carry the fight to his foe. Godfrey smashed two left hooks to the chin and a numbing right to the heart as Risko missed a wild left hook just before the bell.

Round Four
Godfrey, a full head taller than his rival, bored in with all his

heft to plant left and right on Risko's body. Risko pecked with his left and backed away, hurt by Godfrey's tremendous body punches. A storm of lefts and rights to Risko's body almost knocked the white man from his feet. There was tremendous power behind Godfrey's enormous wings. But the Cleveland rubber man, game as a pebble, shot his right to the head and kept everlastingly trying, right up to the bell.

Round Five
As Risko danced in, more cautious now, Godfrey smashed his body with lefts and rights and drew grunts heard back in the dollar seats. Johnny made little impression of the man mountain with his very best blows and Godfrey's long arms easily reached Johnny's body. Godfrey belted the white boy all around the ring with an awful body barrage. Johnny was game, but mighty tired at the gong.

Round Six
Godfrey laid back, content to let Risko carry the burden of the attack and hold when Johnny got dangerous. Risko smashed a left hook full on Godfrey's chin but Big George only smiled. Like a terrier worrying a mastiff, Johnny pounded in and ran smack into a series of short rights to that head that bounced him backward. Johnny beamed to allay the fears of his admirers and came back to the corner smiling at the bell.

Round Seven
Godfrey nearly floored Risko with a hammering left and right to the chin. Johnny backed clear to the ropes arms wound about his head, body crouched in protection. Godfrey let him go and shot a right to the heart as they came back to the cen-

ter of the ring. Risko flinched under a left hook to the body but valiantly hooked his left back at Godfrey's bald head,

Round Eight
Godfrey dueled lefts successfully with Risko, mauling and tugging at close quarters, often separated by the referee. Both slugged to the body. Risko hooked his left clean to the head twice but they were wrestling again at the bell.

Round Nine
Risko never stopped trying, piling into the Negro with left and right swings to the head despite Godfrey's smashes to the body. Johnny slugged big George freely about the head, drove him into a corner for a steady pasting, and the crowd roared as they battled like a pair of dock workers. Johnny belabored Godfrey with both hands, slugging with defense, and absorbed half a dozen counters without a quiver at the gong.

Round Ten
Risko swarmed all over the big Negro, driving him to the ropes under a cloud of swings that came from all directions. Risko buried his left deep in Godfrey's body and George wilted. Godfrey rallied swinging Risko about the ring with his massive arms and shooting his punches short to the body. Johnny never stopped trying, swinging both lefts and rights to the Negro's head. Very tired they leaned heads together and pounded each others ribs while the crowd bellowed encouragement at Risko. They were hauling and tugging at the final gong."

Johnny was scheduled to meet Bearcat Wright on July 13th,

in Omaha. But during a sparring session on July 8th, Risko was butted by his sparring partner, Jeff Baulknight and it opened an old wound over Johnny's left eye. Manager Danny Dunn, wisely called off the fight. Risko was already scheduled to meet South African, Johnny Squires on July 19th so he would need the additional time to make sure his cut healed properly.

On July 20th Risko continued his winning ways taking a 10-round nod over Johnny Squires, South African Champion, in Detroit, Michigan. Prior to the fight the management proclaimed that Johnny Risko was the real champion. He had his followers in Detroit and many felt he was entitled to the decision when he fought Tom Heeney. Of course Heeney got the win and went on to meet Gene Tunney for the heavyweight championship. The glowing tributes about Johnny Risko were all part of the build up to create interest in the match at Navin Field with the South African meeting the Cleveland Baker Boy. Jack Dempsey was obtained as the referee for this contest. The bout originally had been scheduled for July 19th but rain postponed it for a day.

The banner at the head of the *Plain Dealer* sports page (July 21st) boldly read:

"RISKO EASILY OUTPOINTS SQUIRES IN TEN-ROUND SCRAP"

The story from Detroit by Harry Bullion further stated that *"Steady, Two-Fisted Attack Gives Baker Boy Easy Ten-Round Victory."* The text of his column read as follows:

"DETROIT, July 20- Johnny Squires. South African heavyweight, tonight tried the path of many others of the English school in going down to inglorious defeat at the hands of Cleveland Johnny Risko before the gaze of 23,000 people who jammed Navin Field to see the bout and Jack Dempsey.

Dempsey was the attraction and the contest, as poor as it was, only secondary. Risko gave everything he had but the cautious, holding tactics of the Boer had the aggressive Clevelander at a disadvantage, but he won all of the ten rounds, all save the first with plenty to spare.

Squires did not even have aggressiveness to recommend him. He fell into a clinch at every opportunity, and when Risko did manage to get to him at long range he held out a long left hand and usually forced Risko to come in close and almost invariably a clinch would follow.

Squires Takes Beating

There was not a knockdown during the ten rounds, but Squires came out of the bout with the claret flowing from his nose and body that was livid with welts, testimony of the terrific beating he took to the body from the first to the last round.

Risko did not look as good in trouncing Squires as he did in losing a close decision to Tom Heeney here last October, not because the Clevelander was not as good, but because he had a fellow in there who refused to make a fight of it.
Squires appeared unwilling to go along with the pudgy fellow who has been the big stumbling block to enterprising heavy-

weight challengers the past year.

At no stage of the bout did Squires carry the fight to his opponent and after the first round, Risko had more trouble shaking Squires out of clinches than he had in blocking punches. Squires made it close by the use of his long left in the first round but from the second round on, Risko won by himself. He pummeled Squires about the body from the second to the last bell, rocked him with sweeping lefts to the head a half dozen times and on three occasions it appeared Squires was going to the floor, but in each instance, he managed to weather the assault.

Early in the second round, Dempsey warned Squires after he dug his left to Risko's groin, but the Clevelander was not hurt and immediately proceeded to punch Squires across and almost out of the ring.

As early as the fifth round, the crowd was begging Dempsey to throw Squires out of the ring. The big fellow from Johannesburg is a fair boxer with an accurate left hand, but he is much too cautious to get along in the ear tinning business in this country.

Squires did not land a solid punch throughout the bout but with only a few seconds to go in the last round, he cut loose his right and the punch grazed Risko's eye, opening a small wound over the left optic, Risko's only mark of battle.

Dempsey provided all the color the bout carried. The former champion bedecked in white flannels moved about the ring faster than the boxers. He was given a tremendous ovation when he entered the ring and another when he left it. Just before Dempsey instructed the principals, a comely miss presented Risko with a huge bouquet of flowers, a token from Slovak admirers of Detroit."

Quintin Romero Rojas of South America. He and Risko met four times; two for the Cleveland Rubber Man and two 'No Decisions'

New Zealand's Tom Heeney (above - photo courtesy of Dave Cameron) and in action with Risko (below)

Risko on the attack versus Paulino Uzcudun (above) and Jack Sharkey (below). The Cleveland man won both.

"Ain't he a big guy tho!"

Johnny Risko and the giant George Godfrey pose at the weigh-in prior to their 27 June, 1928 bout in New York.

Winning and Losing

After defeating Johnny Squires on July 20th, the Risko fortunes took a different turn. Johnny Risko would stay active the rest of 1928 and continued on into 1929. He would average a fight a month during that time frame. Although he would have some big wins he never won more than two consecutive fights during that period. It seemed that his career would always have those hills and valleys.

Johnny fought a guy named Roberto Roberti on August 15, 1928, in Brooklyn and lost by disqualification in six rounds. On August 13th the odds were 4-1 in favor of Risko but by the day of the fight had dropped to 3-1. At one time the odds had been 7-1 in Risko's favor but some experts felt that the Godfrey fight had taken a lot out of Johnny and suddenly the odds started to slide. Former heavyweight contender, Harry Wills, who had helped the Italian train for the fight also applied for a license to second Roberti.

Although Roberti was almost five inches taller and twenty-five pounds heavier, the experts still felt Johnny Risko would be way too much for the Italian. Writer, Jack Farrell of New York wrote on the 14th, "Italian Seems Due for Real Larruping". And except for the first round Risko did indeed give the Italian Roberti a real drubbing. In the sixth round during a vicious exchange to the body, Roberti suddenly slumped to the canvas. The referee helped Roberti to his corner and immediately declared him the winner on foul, saying that Risko had hit him low in a clinch.

According to Gordon Cobbledick of *The Cleveland Plain Dealer* (8-16-28)

"Few at ringside saw the low blow. They did see Roberti slump and saw Risko tap a light hook to the jaw, a hook that wasn't hard enough by several pounds to topple the giant. It was a half minute before the crowd took in the situation. Then a chorus of mingled boos and cheers sounded."

Ironically that was the third fight in 1928 that Roberti won by a foul. That being said neither Risko nor Danny Dunn protested the decision.

On September 9th the road trip continued in Omaha and Risko won a ten-round decision over Bearcat Wright. Wright was not exactly chopped liver, he won 58 fights in his career with only 17 losses. He won 42 of those contests by kayo. During his career he fought such fighters as Sam Langford, Tiger Jack Fox, George Godfrey and Max Baer. When Jack Johnson hung around way too long, Wright knocked him out in five rounds on April 16, 1928, with a solar plexus punch. November 8, 1928, Johnny went to Fremont, Ohio, and defeated Tut Jackson over the distance of ten rounds. Jackson, who was born James Johnson Jackson in Washington Courthouse, Ohio, like Bearcat Wright had a long career with over 120 fights. But he was strictly a journeyman at best. Most of his 75 wins came against fighters who were not anywhere near being considered contenders. He had defeated Sam Langford once upon a time but the great Langford was near the end of his storied career. He had also lost four out of five against Bearcat Wright with a fifth fight being called a draw.

1,800 viewed the Risko-Jackson scrap as Johnny won eight out of ten rounds. Risko weighed 194 pounds and according to the ringside review *"seemed a trifle slow"*. Risko pretty much pasted Jackson around the ring. Somehow Tut found enough stamina to win the last round, actually trading Risko blow for blow.

On November 30th Johnny traveled to Boston to fight Jim Maloney. Boston was Maloney's hometown so Risko didn't expect any favors. Maloney had been in with a lot of good fighters and had wins over Jack Sharkey, Jack Delaney, Jack DeMave and Jack Renault prior to this contest with Johnny Risko.

Unfortunately for Risko, Jim Maloney turned in one of his best performances. The next day the local stories praised Maloney on his points victory over the Clevelander. They referred to the fight as *"The greatest battle of his career"*. The crowd of 19,000 witnessed Maloney outslug Risko and return to the ranks of heavyweight contender. It was the largest crowd at that time to ever witness an indoor match in Boston and set a record for gate receipts in New England at

$37,386.50. Maloney boxed at long range most of the fight and piled up a huge lead. He took the attack to the body at times and even when Risko landed some big punches, he didn't seem to flinch.

On December 28th Johnny again fought in Boston and lost a decision to Ernie Schaaf. According to the write-ups Schaaf won five rounds, Risko four with one even. Johnny, who came in at 192 lb. one pound lighter than Schaaf, made a gallant effort in the tenth, with a rally that almost pulled it out. He almost dropped Schaaf with terrific lefts and rights to the body. It appeared Risko needed a knockout to win the fight at that stage. However the next day in the local papers James E. Doyle was quoted as saying:

"Johnny Risko got another application of 'the works', as the same are put on the cultured city of Boston...

We have it from our own specially trained investigators over there on the Atlantic seaboard that the Cleveland Bouncer DID whip that Ernie Schaaf person....Even as he whipped Jimmy Maloney in the same ring recently.

Only to see Maloney bag the official nod at the blow-off."
—*The Cleveland Plain Dealer* (12-30-28)

Johnny did defeat Tut Jackson a second time on January 24th. The accounts in the Brooklyn Daily Eagle on February 1, 1929, stated that Risko was hard pressed to get the verdict over Jackson, who in the past before the Risko fight had lost to Harry Wills, who was long finished as a serious contender.

Leading up to the Schmeling fight Johnny obviously

didn't appear to be at the top of his game. Since the winning streak ended with the Squires match, he engaged in six fights and won three and lost three.

Danny Dunn was quoted in the paper as saying *"Too much money."*

He went on to say;

"Yup. John made so much soft dough....all in a bunch...that he didn't think he needed to bother training any more. But now he realizes his mistake and he's goin' to buckle down to bus'ness in earnest, like he used to. As a matter of fact, though...in as rotten shape as he was...he really won those Boston fights with Maloney and Schaaf. The biggest part of the crowd and the majority of the newspaper guys gave him both fights."

Johnny had the body type that even when he was in boxing condition he still looked pudgy. His weight would fluctuate from the 180s to over 200 lbs. for some fights. More often than not the writers had some sort of comment about his body when they were describing his fights.
Schmeling was called "The German Dempsey", because he resembled the former champ in looks, if not in boxing style.

Although the critics claimed Risko had lost a lot of his fire since his tough battle with George Godfrey, most were not jumping on the bandwagon to proclaim Herr Max the upcoming winner in his battle with Risko. They were not sure he could hold up to a constant battering, remembering how he folded against Gypsy Daniels less than a year ago.

Johnny's manager Danny Dunn felt he would be in

his best condition for his fight with Max Schmeling. He felt Johnny was just tired and needed a rest before the big battle. A vacation would be nice but most important to Danny Dunn was that the conditioning of Johnny would be the best possible because he knew a win over the German would surely put Risko back in the title hunt.

Max Schmeling (above left) with Johnny Risko

Max Schmeling

Although some critics would write in their columns that Johnny Risko's star had faded or was fading, it still is important to note that when Germany's Max Schmeling was scheduled to meet Cleveland's Johnny Risko on February 1, 1929, in New York, it was still considered a big test for Herr Schmeling.

Prior to World War II Schmeling had the distinction of winning the Heavyweight Championship while laying on the deck after being fouled by Jack Sharkey, in 1930. He also defended that title in Cleveland, Ohio, on July 3, 1931, with a fifteen round technical knockout of Young Stribling. That fight was the first event ever held in the then spanking new Cleveland Municipal Stadium, which had a seating capacity of over 80,000. Then on June 21, 1932, Schmeling lost the title to Jack Sharkey in a very controversial decision.

Of course most people who know anything about boxing are familiar with his two bouts against Joe Louis. Max unfairly became part of the propaganda machine of Nazi Germany, prior to and during World War II.

The Max Schmeling story of course didn't start there. He had to work his way up the ladder like any other fighter. And it didn't always come easy for the fighter later called *"The Black Uhlan"* by his then American manager, Joe Jacobs. Max Schmeling was born on September 28, 1905, in Klein Luckow, Germany. He turned pro in 1924, around the same time as Johnny Risko. Under his first manager, Arthur Bulow he fought all of his early bouts in Europe, mostly in Germany. He fought at light-heavy in the beginning and could not be considered a juggernaut as he was stopped twice in the early years while racking up wins against mostly no-name fighters. He got stopped by a TKO in the 4th round against Max Diekmann in Berlin, on October 4th in only his fifth career fight. In 1925 he lost to someone named Jack Taylor, a globe-trotting American journeyman and was held to a draw against Leon Randol in Brussels. Then he was stopped in the second round by a quality fighter in Larry Gains.

In 1926 Schmeling was held to a draw by the same Max Diekmann who had stopped him. A few fights later Max fought for the German Light Heavyweight Title against Diekmann and won the championship with a first round kayo. This bout took place on August 24th in Berlin.

1927 was a very good year for Max Schmeling as he fought 15 times and won all of them, including 13 knockouts. He added the European Light Heavyweight Title to his resume when he knocked out Fernand DeLarge in the 14th round in Dortmund on June 19th. On November 6th he defended his new title with a 7th round kayo over Hein Domogergen in Leipzig. On December 2nd he closed out the year with a decision win over Gypsy Daniels of Wales.

1928 started out in fine fashion as he defended his European Light Heavyweight Title with a first round knockout over Michele Bonaglia, in Berlin. Then he was stunned when he was stopped in the opening stanza against Gypsy Daniels in Frankfurt, Germany. Max regrouped and won his next two fights, including adding the German Heavyweight Title to his name when he won a 15-round decision over Franz Diener, in Berlin on April 4th. He also took on a new manager when he hooked up with the previously mentioned, Joe Jacobs. Joe Jacobs whose nickname was *"Yussel the Muscle"* by local scribes, was very controversial to say the least. Some would say Jacobs was the quintessential boxing manager of the 1920s and 1930s. He was usually seen chomping on a cigar. He was streetwise, combative, fast-talking and also called a "schmoozer". His critics would say Jacobs knew nothing about boxing, but he knew how to wheel and deal and get his fighters the best possible matches.

When Max Schmeling won the vacant heavyweight championship over Jack Sharkey in June of 1930, it was Jacobs who jumped into the ring screaming "foul" until the confused referee disqualified the Boston gob.

When Schmeling lost the title on the controversial decision to Sharkey, in 1932, it was Jacobs who coined the phrase "We wuz robbed!"

Later on during the Nazis drive to power Jacobs got involved in demonstrations and was even seen giving the Nazi salute. Max Schmeling would later be pressured by the Nazis to dump his Jewish manager but he refused. However there was an even greater uproar in the United States, especially in the Jewish communities, when photographs of Jacobs giving the Nazi salute were published.

Prior to all of the controversy and winning the title

Jacobs did however land three fights for Schmeling in the United States. On November 23, 1928, he defeated Joe Monte in New York via an 8th round kayo. Starting 1929 off in good form, he won a decision over Joe Sekyra, in ten rounds, on January 4th, also in New York. On January 22nd he knocked out Pietro Corri in Newark, New Jersey.

So some people felt Johnny Risko was finished, not a contender and would not be a factor in the heavyweight division. However the powers that be thought Schmeling had to defeat a fighter such as Risko to earn a title shot. It was called Max's biggest test and could make him or break him as a title contender. The great writer Damon Runyon was one of the people who felt the match was important, as stated in a story written on February 1st in New York; "Runyon Sees Go as German's Big Test". He went on to further say he was reserving his opinion on Schmeling until he got by the fading Rubber Man. At the weigh-in Johnny weighed 190 lb. and Max 185 lb.

John Kieran wrote in the New York Times, the day of the fight that "Either Risko had slipped badly the last eight months or he had been anchored, and the parade has gone right by him."

The match set for February 1, 1929, in New York would prove historic for both men and their careers. The story from the following day in The Coshocton Tribune appeared exactly as printed below:

"The Coshocton Tribune
2 Feb 1929

Max Schmelling (sic), German Dempsey, Decisively Defeats

Johnny Risko
NEW YORK, Feb 2
It takes a great man to beat a very good man and Johnny Risko, with the heart of a lion and the jaw of a gorilla, was as good as ever he was last night when, reeling and punch poisoned he was called out on, his feet after a minute and five seconds of the ninth round by a humane referee. Yes, John was very good, very good, but Max Schmeling, the German, was so much better that he actually was greatness itself as he punched Risko until he was silly, leaving nothing Referee Arthur Donovan to do but award the Dempsey of the Deutschland's what is said to be the first legitimate knockout ever scored at Risko's expense.

Four times he had Risko on the axminster and not another man in the ring today would have arisen from the second and third knockdowns which were perfect bull's-eyes, but Risko has the chin of all chins and so he got up and fought back heroically. He still was striking out blindly at his tormentor with the fighting instinct of the true fighting man, although barely able to keep his feet, when the referee wisely decided that too much was a great plenty. He saved this amazing brave man from an actual knockout since it was inevitable that even this glove swallower never was destined to see the tenth and final round.

The fight was nothing less than a ring masterpiece, a saga of glorious courage that filled the eye and gladdened the heart. Risko furnished much of this with his last game stand against the inevitable but it must be admitted that it was the great fighter and not the very good one who turned in the performance that sent the witnesses gibbering out into the night. He did things in this fight that left not the slightest doubt of his greatness. No other kind of a fighter could have taken the mauling Risko gave him thru the third, fourth, fifth and sixth rounds and then, with a single punch in the seventh, practically ruin a man like John for the remainder of the evening.

No other kind of fighter, not even the old Dempsey, could have put a faster and neater finish to a man than Schmeling did in the ninth and last round, This was master workmanship, no less. The witnesses rushed the ringside when it was all over to babble incoherently about "the next champion of the world" and frankly, there was nothing that could be vouchsafed against it.

Incidentally, the young man knows something about keeping the old potato protected, as Risko discovered after casting five hundred rights and lefts at it thru the first seven rounds. John wasn't casting anything after that except possibly a weary eye at his corner. It was an epic sight to see this remarkable punch catcher being beaten down and even unbiased newspapermen were so carried out of their customary lethargy as to wave frantically at him to quit before he was badly hurt.

But there never was any quit in Johnny Risko and he didn't mean to begin last night. No less thrilling was the picture of the cool, yet venomous Schmeling as he calculatingly made his "kill" businesslike. He cut Risko down more rapidly than the writer ever has seen a fighter finished, except by a one punch knockout. And nobody scores that kind against

Johnny Risko. "
After the Risko win Max would go on to defeat Paulino Uzcudun on June 27th, in New York, and get his title fight with Sharkey. Max, after losing the title to Sharkey on June 21, 1932, beat the great middleweight, Mickey Walker by kayo in eight rounds on September 26th. Then in the battle of two Maxes, Schmeling was knocked out by Max Baer in ten rounds, June 8, 1933, in New York. Still Max fought on and eventually landed his first fight with Joe Louis that would forever put him in the annals of boxing history. His June 19, 1936, knockout of Joe Louis, in the 12th round, was a huge victory for Max and Nazi Germany. Adolph Hitler and Propaganda Minister Joseph Goebbels, would use the victory over Louis to promote their "Master Race" theories. Max as often written, never officially joined the Nazi party. How much he was involved in the whole part of world history has been written about many times. There are also many opinions pro and con about his involvement.

When Joe Louis destroyed Schmeling in one round on June 22, 1938, it was a huge victory for Louis and America. War was near and this victory was a devastating defeat for the Nazis. Although there are stories about Schmeling attending Nazi Party rallies after this, he apparently fell out of favor after the Louis defeat and was drafted into the German Army. While serving as a paratrooper in Crete, in 1941, he was injured. After the war he rarely talked about his years during Nazi Germany's reign. He was credited however with saving the lives of two Jewish children, the sons of an old friend, when he hid them in his suite in Berlin's Excelsior Hotel, during "Kristallnacht".

After the war Max was said to be broke and launched

an unsuccessful boxing comeback in 1947. Eventually with the help of friends he was able to buy into a Coca-Cola distributorship and became very wealthy. He also was considered a national hero, one of the few after World War II, in Germany.

Also after the war, Max was blocked from entering the United States, mainly because of the strong influence of American Veterans groups. Finally in 1954, he received a visa. A British military court earlier had cleared Schmeling of any serious Nazi involvement. He eventually became very good friends with Joe Louis and visited him several times. It was said he paid for Louis' medical expenses when times were hard and for his funeral. Max died in 2005, in Wenzendorf, Germany, at age 99.

This author corresponded with Max Schmeling a few times and was surprised that although I typed my letters in English, the return letters came back to me in German. It took a little bit of work to read them as I am not fluent in German. Still a thrill however.

The Risko win will always be considered the springboard to Schmeling landing a title shot by those who followed boxing closely during those years. The Risko-Schmeling fight was The Ring Magazine "Fight of the Year".

Post Schmeling 1929-30

After the Schmeling defeat it was obvious that Johnny Risko had once again lost an opportunity to land a world title shot. Although he showed his heroics in the battle with the German, he also seemed to leave a lot of doubt whether he could ever climb over that last major hurdle to warrant a championship fight.

Risko took two months off and then Danny Dunn lined him up to fight Otto von Porat, the 1924 Olympic Gold Medal winner at the Summer Olympics. The Swedish born Norwegian had won 9 out of his previous 10 bouts, leading up to the Risko match, including victories over Chuck Wiggins and Tom Heeney. Their bout scheduled for April 5, 1929, in Boston, turned out to be a good comeback fight for Risko as he pounded his way to a unanimous decision over his 6' 4" opponent.

The headline in the Chicago Tribune on April 6th told of how the Cleveland Baker Boy had broken his chain of bad luck in Boston with a very aggressive attack that left no doubt who was the winner after ten rounds, as 12,000 fans witnessed the match.

On May 7th Risko was matched with Emmett Rocco, a New Castle, Pa. fighter who accepted an offer of $1500 to fight Johnny (Risko was guaranteed $5,000), which raised a negative response from Boxing Chairman Ed Barry. Rocco had appeared in early March and defeated Al Friedman of Philadelphia before a small local crowd. Barry felt if Rocco was any good he wouldn't accept an amount as small as $1500 to fight Risko. Dan Taylor, who had taken over the matchmaking after Matt Hinkel had semi-retired, continued to present the fight proposal to Chairman Barry. Finally he guaranteed Barry that the fight would be a good one and if not he would resign as matchmaker.

Emmett Rocco

The results as quoted by Dan Taylor in his 1952, Cleveland Press series:

"To make a long story short, the bout turned out to be one of the best heavyweight fights seen here. Rocco upset the dope by getting Referee Frankie Van's decision, although he didn't deserve it; the show drew a capacity crowd of 10,200 with gate receipts of $21,000 and it showed a a profit of nearly $6,000."

Risko's next two bouts turned out to be real duds. Risko usually used a body attack to slow down his opponents, normally he got away with such tactics and they would lead to some of his major victories. But in Boston on June 17th, he fought George Cook, a 5' 9" Australian globe-trotter, who fought all over the world during his career including: Australia, New Zealand, England, France, Germany, Argentina, Italy, South Africa, Canada and the United States. Risko was winning every round. He was disqualified in the 5th round when the referee ruled that he dropped Cook with a low right hook.

Next Johnny was originally supposed to box Jim Maloney in a return match, but Maloney suffered a bad cut in training so Gerald Ambrose "Tuffy" Griffith was substituted. On June 27, 1929, Johnny went in against Tuffy Griffiths in Detroit. His bad luck continued as he once again lost by disqualification, this time in the 7th round. Griffith, whose name often appeared as Griffiths, was winning by a slight margin when the bout ended. Griffith had complained several times when Risko attacked his body. The referee, Al Day had warned Johnny a half dozen times until he stopped the fight in favor of Griffiths. Johnny who had received a nice hand when entering the ring, got booed on the way out.

Risko got a return match with Emmett Rocco on July

29th. Many felt Johnny had been robbed of a decision in their previous fight. Risko left no doubt this time as he won 10 out of the 12 rounds and won the decision of Referee Patsy Halley of New York. More than 7,000 fans sat in the hot Public Hall to see Risko, in great shape at 187 pounds, turn in one of his better performances.

One of the strangest matches locally happened next when Akron's old warrior, Meyer K.O. Christner was approved as an opponent for Risko at Public Hall on September 4th. Christner had fought many of the same fighters Risko had met including Joe Sekyra, Jack Sharkey, Paulino Uzcudun and Otto von Porat. But he was 33 years old, at the time considered very old for a fighter, and had met some of the same men as Risko. Johnny however had won against those opponents and Christner hadn't.

Most people had no doubts Risko would take the measure of the Akron based Christner. 9,838 showed up to witness the match. Risko's share of the gate was $7,881 and K.O. got $7,165. For whatever reason boxing Chairman, Ed Barry kept importing gray-haired Patsy Haley as referee for many of the bigger main events. As a result of his work that night the ending of the fight turned out to be bizarre at best. Johnny was in the process of giving Christner a real beating when suddenly Haley stopped the fight and disqualified Risko for butting. The fans were dumbfounded. There was a lot of shock and puzzlement from both sides of the ring. Christner had been guilty of almost every foul known. Just seconds before Risko was disqualified, Christner had tried to choke Johnny in a clinch. Christner's foul tactics had turned Risko into a wild man in the early going and it lasted until the 9th round when Haley suddenly put a stop to the match.

The fans became so upset with Haley that he had to have a police escort to the dressing room. To add insult to injury Risko was later fined $1,000 by the boxing commission for the foul. Christner escaped with the tainted victory and no fines.

On October 22, 1929, Johnny Risko again returned to Boston, a place that had not been too kind to him. Jim Maloney's cut had healed and they finally were set for their rematch. Risko had a reputation for often avenging defeats in rematches and the Maloney fight proved no different. Johnny was in great shape and simply took Maloney apart, dropping him five different times before referee, Kid McPartland, halted the slaughter in the second round.

The fight started with Risko driving Maloney across the ring and into the ring pole. After the fight Maloney would claim he never recovered from hitting his head. The second round started and Risko hit Maloney with another left hook and had him staggering around the ring. Then Risko cut loose with left and rights and Maloney went down twice for counts of two and once for a four count. He eventually hit the deck again just as the bell rang. Referee, McPartland helped Maloney to his corner and then halted the fight on a TKO. It was a sweet victory for Johnny. The Maloney victory sent Johnny Risko into another rematch with a fighter who had previously defeated him, Ernie Schaaf.

Ernie Schaaf, who later in his career would become a ring fatality, had been a promising up and coming contender. After Matt Hinkel's retirement as matchmaker, Dan Taylor, who took over the reigns, received word that Phil Schlossberg, manager of Ernie Schaaf, had accepted terms for a rematch for a Risko bout in Cleveland. Taylor had been negotiating with Schlossberg for a couple months, eventually signing Jim Maloney, when he couldn't pin down Schlossberg. It turned out Schlossberg and Schaaf had gone on a month long vacation and had never received the contract proposal until after Risko had met Maloney on October 22, 1929.

Schaaf, who was only 21, was considered one of the best of all of the young heavyweights, having won a ten round unanimous decision over Risko the previous December, in Boston. That win did not come easy for Schaaf, who lost three teeth in the 10th round from the rampaging Rubber Man. It was said he swallowed them and almost choked on them at the end. If that had happened in the early going, who knows what could have happened.

As mentioned previously Johnny Risko more than a few times was a much better fighter in return matches with opponents who had defeated him. It proved true in this return match with Schaaf. 11,197 fans jammed Public Hall to see as exciting battle as witnessed in a long time. Both fighters were hurt during the contest, with Schaaf being on the verge of a knockout at the end of the seventh round with a left to the body and a right to the jaw. The bell saved him as he staggered to the corner. In the tenth round several right hands from Schaaf had Risko staggering but he weathered the storm. Typical of the endless recuperative powers of the Cleveland Baker Boy, he came roaring back in the eleventh to land lethal punches that had Schaaf in trouble several times. In the twelfth round they traded punches throughout but Johnny had the best of it. When the bell sounded at the end, Johnny Risko had clearly won this fight all by himself.

A return match with Tuffy Griffiths was secured for December 27, 1929, in Madison Square Garden, New York. According to manager Danny Dunn, if Risko would defeat Griffths, he was in line for a return match with Jack Sharkey. Unfortunately he didn't win the fight, in fact Risko lost most of the rounds while losing a unanimous decision. Griffiths did everything in this battle except knock out Risko. However Risko brought the crowd to its feet in the eighth and ninth rounds with a furious rally. In the tenth round Griffiths took back the offensive and fought tooth and nail, giving as much as he got. The decision was never in question.

On January 20, 1930, the road warrior came back to Cleveland for a match with Italian heavyweight, Riccardo Bertazzolo, who could be considered an "opponent" at best. The match was one-sided in Johnny's favor. He floored Bertazzolo in the seventh round. The headline in the Plain Dealer the next day said it all, "Risko's Steady Fire Drubs Bertazzolo In All 10 Rounds".

Risko's next venture in the ring was against the giant, Victorio Campolo, from Quilmes, Buenos Aires, Argentina. Campolo, who was born in Reggio Calabria, Italy, in 1903, was listed at 6' 9" tall and was said to have an 86 inch reach. His nickname was 'El Gigante de Quilmes' - The Giant of Quilmes. The writers in New York said he was much too big for "Tiny" Risko. What the writers didn't mention however was the size of Johnny Risko's heart.

On February 27th, Risko and Campolo met in a 10-round contest in Miami, Florida. Prior to the fight they measured Campolo and said he was closer to 6' 6" tall. Still he had a lot of height and reach on Johnny. At the weigh-in Johnny was 195 and Campolo 226. But it didn't matter. All this talk about Risko being too small for Campolo really didn't become a big factor. The writers, including Damon Runyon mentioned that Risko appeared a foot shorter than Campolo. Still after a bit of a shaky start Johnny took the fight to Campolo.

At the end most agreed that Johnny Risko won 8 out of 10 rounds, with Campolo winning the first and the tenth. Although Risko won the Campolo fight, some didn't feel he was his old self. A return match was set up for New York at Madison Square Garden, on March 24, 1930. Fans of the big man from Argentina felt their man looked great in the gym. Unfortunately that did not carry over to the actual fight. Risko won again, although Campolo landed the heavier blows. It seemed Campolo was reluctant to lead or start an attack. The final decision had referee Arthur Donovan and one of the judges voting for Risko and the other casting his vote for Campolo. Not only was the Argentine battler not willing to lead an attack, he was also warmed several times by Donovan for illegal rabbit punches. However after the fight, the majority of writers and ringsiders polled felt Campolo should have been given the verdict over Cleveland's Rubber Man. It was also revealed after the contest that Risko had hurt his right shoulder in the eighth round.

Risko took almost three months off to let his shoulder heal. On May 5, 1930, Johnny married the former Margaret Yoder of Shaker Heights, Ohio; Johnny was 27 and Margaret 20. Then Dunn signed him to fight the big Basque, Paulino Uzcudun for a second time, on June 19, 1930, this time in Detroit. In a Cleveland Plain Dealer special report on June 19th, it stated Johnny had just returned from a honeymoon trip and most likely wasn't in the best of shape. Risko put on another very strong performance as he won eight out of ten rounds, almost stopping the Basque in the fifth round. Uzcudun staged a furious rally in round six and landed some stinging punches with both hands. Risko's fighting heart came into play as he hung on to survive the round. The crowd was really into it and pulling for the Spaniard, although his rally was short lived. 11,000 fans cheered as Risko's attack picked up and he won the remaining rounds. Paulino may have won the second and sixth but that was all he could tally. Risko had cut Uzcudun's left eye in the third round, eventually closing it completely in the ninth stanza. He also inflicted damage to his right eye.

Johnny had a couple fighters who seemed to give him more trouble during his career than others. Tuffy Griffiths was one such fighter. Griffiths, from Sioux city, Iowa, was a heavyweight contender who had beaten Risko twice previously when they were signed for a July 2, 1930, bout in Chicago. Johnny Risko would always be known as a "spoiler" who wrecked many contenders aspirations during his career. Heading into his third match with Tuffy, Johnny had only received one real decisive defeat in his career, the Schmeling technical knockout the previous year.

Griffiths started quickly and easily won the first five rounds. Although as the fight continued his punches seemed to lose steam. However he hurt Risko badly in round eight and was the winner at the end without any doubt.

Risko had two major bouts postponed and then canceled during the months of July and August. First a rematch with Ton Heeney scheduled for July 17th, was postponed and then canceled in July when Johnny re-injured his right shoulder during training. Then a match with Ernie Schaaf, scheduled for early August was canceled, first because of weather and then because of poor ticket sales.

While Risko could be called the "Spoiler of Contenders", he also could be called " John The Giant Killer". He never was afraid to fight anyone and many times he did take on men who were a lot taller and many pounds heavier. On September 16, 1930, he took on 6' 4" Babe Hunt in Oklahoma City. Hunt had defeated James Braddock and Ernie Schaaf previous to the Risko match. Johnny did not turn out to be a "Giant Killer" in the Hunt contest as Babe utilized his long jab, and seemed to have Risko puzzled by it. Perhaps the best round of the fight was the tenth where both fighters slugged it out. At the end the referee, Ed Cocbrane, of Kansas City, and the two judges all voted for Hunt. At the finish Risko appeared battered and tired according to reports.

The disqualification bugaboo continued to haunt Johnny in his next bout.

On October 23, 1930, he met Dick Daniels at Boston. Like many of his previous losses on foul, Risko was winning the Daniels fight handily. When his punches went south of the border in round seven, the fight was halted. Risko's manager Danny Dunn said, "Sure, he's lost on a foul before, but this one was the most costly lesson of the lot. We were supposed to get $5,000, but under the rules over there we don't get a nickel on a low blow."

On November 7th Johnny went back to Detroit, this time meeting the former great Middleweight Champ, Mickey Walker over ten rounds. Walker had moved up in weight and although not the great fighter he was at middleweight, was still a fighting force. Risko and Walker engaged in a close match. Mickey worked the body with left hooks and more than a few times made Risko wince. The huge crowd had to admire Walker as he gave away more than twenty-five pounds to Risko. The match was a very good one with lots of action and the crowd roared its approval. Walker pulled out the tenth round which eliminated any doubt. When referee Al Day raised Walker's arm, the crowd gave both men a big ovation. Most experts felt that although Walker fought a very good fight, he was not heavyweight championship material. For Risko it was another setback.

As 1930 was coming to an end Risko went back to Boston to meet Jim Maloney for the third time, on December 5th. In Maloney's previous fight he had defeated Primo Carnera. Just when many probably thought Johnny Risko was finished as a force in the heavyweight division he again fooled them when he staged a wild closing rally to take the close decision over Maloney. The local papers referred to the contest as "A furious ten-round slugging match". Risko weighed 195 pounds and Maloney 196.

Contending Again 1931-32

During his 1930 December victory over Jim Maloney in Boston, Risko incurred a badly bruised left elbow. It kept him out of action for three weeks. On February 6, 1931, he returned to action in Detroit, against Charley Retzlaff, a pretty good heavyweight from Duluth, Minnesota. It did not go well. 14,000 fans watched as Retzlaff uncorked numerous right hands to the head of the Cleveland Rubber Man, building up a huge lead that was never threatened although Risko was always trying hard for the knockout right till the end. 1931 was not off to a great start. To add insult to injury prior to the bout with Retzlaff, a warrant was issued for Risko's arrest by Lakewood (Ohio) Municipal Court. He had failed to appear in answer to a police summons for speeding down Clifton Boulevard, January 30th, with his bride. That was not the first nor last time Johnny got stopped for speeding or reckless driving.

On February 25th Johnny got a return match with the great Mickey Walker, this time in Miami. He hoped to avenge his earlier defeat against the former middleweight champ. Although he had a 30 pound weight advantage he allowed Walker to steal the fight with a great finish in the last two rounds to gain the judges verdict. 20,000 people watched. The next day after the fight an editorial appeared in the *Cleveland Plain Dealer* (2-27-31) regarding the Walker bout. It appeared exactly as shown below:

"On the Chin Again

Johnny Risko takes it on the chin again. His defeat by Mickey Walker in Miami Wednesday night was a disappointment to his Cleveland friends who had been hoping the local baker boy would return to his old-time form.

Not long ago Johnny was regarded as a likely heavyweight champion. His stock has fallen rapidly in the recent deflation period, and after the defeat by Walker many will be inclined to remove it from the tape.

Johnny, however, is still young and has great natural ability. But if he hopes to get anywhere in the fight business he must take himself and his work more seriously.

Rich foods and high powered motor cars are Johnny's major weaknesses. Both are serious obstacles in the way of a professional athlete. Unless Johnny can take the fat off his neck and resist the temptation to step so hard on the accelerator his career as a fighter will neither be long nor bright.

In the active heavyweight ring at the present time there is probably not another fighter who has the natural ability, or the punch which Johnny packs. But Johnny gets nowhere because he is content with the small measure of success he has already achieved and the financial reward that goes with it.

After losing to Walker his purse is but little fatter, and his reputation as a fighter is at low ebb. It behooves Johnny Risko to get in shape and do the fighting of which is capable, or to go back to the bakery."

A month later on March 25, 1931, in St. Louis, Johnny met Missouri native, John Schwake. " Risko Scores Point Decision Over Schwake" bellowed a headline in the St. Louis Times after the fight. But this bout ended with one of the newspaper decisions of the era and the bout was given to Schwake. However Sports Editor, Dick Farrington, of the St. Louis Times, was quoted: "John Schwake was outscored, out-held and outfoxed by Johnny Risko." (Cleveland Plain Dealer 3-26-31).

March 30th Johnny went back to Madison Square Garden in New York to meet young heavyweight Stanley Poreda of Jersey City, New Jersey. The result of this contest was no better than his previous 1931 efforts to date, as he lost a decision in ten rounds. Writer James P Dawson scored it six rounds for Poreda, three rounds for Risko and one even. Basically Poreda used superior boxing to carve out the victory. Risko tried to bull rush him at times and had him a bit miffed but the youngster regained his composure and went back to boxing at a distance to secure the victory. It was his biggest to date. Sadly a ringside guest of Poreda, Rudy Hasse, 50, apparently could not handle the excitement and died of a heart attack.

Risko's 1927 loss to Tom Heeney often is stated as the fight that most likely ruined Johnny's best chance at a title shot. On April 6th, Risko finally got the New Zealander back into the ring as they met in Toronto, California. The crowd of 5,500 was not too enthused as they booed in the early stages. Risko put on a brisk rally in the closing rounds to gain a unanimous decision from all three judges. Risko had a 19-pound disadvantage to the 209 1/2 pound "Hard Rock", but managed to stagger him a few times. Once again Johnny had avenged a previous defeat.

On April 21, 1931, Risko squared off with King Levinsky in Boston. The heading in a special to the *Cleveland Plain Dealer* the next day stated:

"JOHNNY WINS EVERY ONE OF TEN SESSIONS.

Rubber Guy Plays Tattoo on King's Body as He Breezes in"

According to the ringside reports Risko used a strong body attack that at times lifted the Chicago fighter off his feet. He never let up from start to finish. Occasionally Johnny would shift his attack to the head and indeed raised a lump over Levinsky's eye.

On May 5th future heavyweight champion, Max Baer came in from California to meet Risko. Baer had knocked out most of his opponents with his big right hand.

Prior to meeting Johnny, he had been out-boxed over ten rounds by Tommy Loughran, in New York. Baer and

Risko were supposed to be matched earlier on in New York but for some reason the bout couldn't be locked in as Baer's camp claimed they needed more time to train. Risko had been very disappointed when Baer pulled out of the fight and looked forward to finally meeting him. The bout was set for Public Hall and "The Livermore Larruper", as he was called, bragged that he would have no problem with Cleveland's Rubber Man.

Baer, 22, was being touted as a future heavyweight champion and most experts felt he would get by the veteran. He and the fans would be in for a surprise. When the fight ended Risko's hand was raised in victory.

Here is how the fight went as written in the *Cleveland Plain Dealer* on May 6th:

"Fight By Rounds

ROUND 1- They sparred in the center of the ring. Baer jabbed with a left and crossed a right to the head. They clinched and sparred again. Risko's left hook went off Baer's nose. Risko hooked a left to the jaw and the crowd cheered. Baer jabbed two lefts to the nose. Risko jabbed a left to the body then looped a left to Baer's neck. Baer crossed two hard rights to the jaw. Up close, Baer shook Risko with a volley of rights to the jaw and ear. Risko brought up a short left and right to the jaw and the crowd cheered. They were sparring at the bell.

ROUND 2- Risko ripped a left to the body and Baer drove a right to the ribs. They traded left jabs and then Risko planted a fine left to the jaw. Baer missed with a haymaking left and

Risko put a right to the jaw at close quarters. Baer grinned as they clinched. Risko jabbed a left to the body and jaw and Baer shot a right to the jaw. Risko's left went around Baer's head as they clinched. Risko ducked under a left and they clinched. Risko rushed in with rights and lefts to the body. They traded rights up close and Risko had the advantage. Now Baer put three short rights to the jaw. Risko looped a left to the nose just before the round ended.

ROUND 3- Risko was short with a left and they sparred. Baer popped a light left to the ribs and jabbed two lefts to the mouth. Risko jabbed a left to the body. Baer put a good left and right to the body. As they punched in a clinch, Risko slapped a left to the nose and they clinched again. Baer crossed a hard right to the jaw and Risko retreated. Then Johnny rushed back with lefts and rights to the body. Risko had the edge as they mixed viciously in a neutral corner. Risko outfought Baer up close, putting a hard right to the Californian's jaw. Johnny was still out punching the Californian at close quarters as the bell rang.

ROUND 4- Baer rushed and they clinched. They swapped left jabs. After a clinch Baer drove two good rights to the body and jabbed a pair of stiff lefts to the face. Risko jabbed to the nose and body. Baer hooked a left to the stomach. Risko covered up as Baer punched and then laced the Californian's ribs with lefts and rights. They clinched near the ropes. Risko put a left-looper to the jaw. They punched evenly in a clinch. Risko lopped a left to the ear. Baer's left hook glanced off Risko's nose. They were punching up close at the bell.

ROUND 5- Baer jabbed a left to the nose and crossed a right to the ear. Risko jabbed a left to the body and nose. Baer smashed a right to the head and Risko a left to the body. Risko jabbed a left to the chin. Baer outpunched Risko in a clinch. Risko jabbed a left to the nose and they clinched once more. Baer tapped a left and right to the head. As Risko jabbed a left to the nose, Baer brought up a hard right to the body. Baer crossed a right to the head. Up close Baer shook Risko with a left and right to the jaw. Johnny retaliated with a right and left to the jaw, not so hard and another left. Baer hooked a left to the nose. Baer outfought Risko as they milled at close range. They were going fast at the bell.

ROUND 6- Baer charged out punching for the body, and they clinched. They sparred and clinched again. Baer jabbed two lefts to the nose. Risko jabbed a left to the mouth and Baer hooked a hard left to the jaw. Up close, Risko slammed lefts and rights to the body. Each crossed a right to the jaw. They traded left jabs and clinched. Baer out-punched Risko up close. Johnny had the advantage at longer range. Baer put a right to the body and Risko landed a right to the jaw. Baer's right glanced off Risko's head and they clinched. Risko blocked Baer's punches and slammed lefts and rights to Max's body as the round came to a close.

ROUND 7 - Baer crossed a right to the head. Then he put a left and right to the body. Risko jabbed two lefts to the face and they clinched. Risko hooked a left to the jaw and they clinched. Risko jabbed a left to the mouth and clinched. Baer hooked a short right to the body. Each punched to the body in a clinch. Risko jabbed a left to the nose and Baer shot a short a right to the ribs. Risko blocked Baer's punches to the body and scored good lefts and rights to Max's body and jaw. Risko jabbed a left to the nose and Baer crossed a right to the ear. There was much rough clinching now. And they were coming out of these scrimmages at the bell.

ROUND 8- Baer's right grazed Risko's head. Risko sent a right to the body. Baer almost wrestled Johnny to the floor in a clinch. Risko put a left and right to the jaw. Baer out-punched Johnny in a clinch. Risko jabbed a left to the nose and body and Baer hooked a right to the stomach. Risko shook Baer with a good left and right to the jaw. Baer slapped a left to the head and Risko rapped a right to the ear. Risko crossed a good right to the jaw, but was outpunched by Baer in another clinch. Baer's head went back as Risko jabbed two lefts. Risko looped a left to the jaw and Baer a left to the ear. Risko landed a light right to the jaw as the bell rang.

ROUND 9- They traded jabs and clinched, each punching to the body. Baer jabbed a left to the jaw. Risko looped a left to the jaw. Risko hooked a left to the jaw and Baer crossed a right to the ear. Risko hooked a left to the jaw and Baer crossed a right to the jaw. They sparred, then clinched. They sparred and clinched again. Risko jabbed a left to the nose. Risko was wild with a left, but followed with a right that reached Baer's jaw. After a clinch, Risko slammed lefts and rights to the jaw and the crowd cheered. Now Risko brought up two good rights the the jaw. Baer hooked a right and left to the body. Risko was outmauling Baer at close quarters when the bell sounded.

ROUND 10- They sparred under the center lights. Baer jabbed a left to the nose and hooked a left to the ribs. Up close, Baer put a right-left to the body. Baer wrestled Risko to the floor in a clinch and the crowd booed the Californian. Risko hooked a left to the ribs. Risko jabbed two lefts to the nose and followed with a left to the body. They traded left jabs and clinched. Risko belted a left and right to the body. Baer had the edge as they punched in a clinch. Risko shook Baer with two rights to the jaw. Baer outrushed Johnny in a clinch. Each scored with rights and lefts to the body. Risko brought up three short rights to the jaw as Baer punched to the stomach. Risko took a left to the stomach as the fight ended."

The next fight card Johnny Risko would be involved with was rather historic. On July 3, 1931, the brand new Cleveland Municipal Stadium was opening to an event for the first time. Some say the huge stadium (80,000 plus) was built to lure the 1932 Olympics to Cleveland. This has never been proven. What did happen, however, was a heavyweight championship fight. Cleveland with the help of Cleveland News Boxing Writer, Dan Taylor and Damon Runyon, No. 1 boxing and feature writer for the Hearst newspapers, somehow convinced officials of Madison Square Garden, Joe Jacobs, manager of Schmeling and everyone else involved, that the new stadium would be the ideal place to hold Schmeling's defense. The promoters were hoping for a huge crowd in the mammoth stadium. Unfortunately only 37,396 witnessed Schmeling stop the outgunned Stribling with a 15th round technical knockout.

Johnny Risko was matched with Tony Galento of Orange, New Jersey, in an eight round match, following the world championship. The fight was rough and hard, each man swinging wildly at times. Galento known as "Two Ton Tony" throughout most of his career, weighed 229 compared to 185 for Risko. Years later Tony Galento wrote in A Farewell To Heroes, "I beat Johnny Risko in ten rounds..I could have knocked him out, only I had sore hands, and I was afraid to let one go too hard for fear I might break my hand, but I could feel him go weak a couple times when I hit him." Of course anyone who followed Galento's career knows he always had some excuse for losing and usually claimed he won fights he actually didn't.

On August 4, 1931, Johnny Risko met up again with Akron's K.O. Christner. The previous time they fought most observers believed Christner was guilty of every foul known to man, yet Risko was the one who got disqualified in the 9th round. They were scheduled for a 12-rounder at the Taylor Bowl on Harvard Avenue, in Newburg Heights, Ohio. According to the write-up in the Cleveland Plain Dealer by James Doyle, "Johnny won ten rounds out of twelve and had K.O. on the verge of dreamland in the 12th and final round."

Philadelphia was the site for a third match with Tommy Loughran, set for October 19th. The light-heavyweight champion had previously defeated Risko twice, once in 1926 and once in 1927. Using a darting left he made it three in row over Johnny as he built up a huge lead in the first seven rounds before coming down off of his toes in the last three rounds. This allowed Risko to inflict some damage. Still Loughran weighing 188 had too much ring speed and boxing ability to allow the 198 pound Risko to get in many solid licks.

Max Baer and his manager had been seeking a return match with Risko ever since the decision loss in Cleveland the previous May. Baer got his wish on November 9, 1931, in San Francisco when they were signed for a 10-rounder. This time it was a different kind of fight for Risko. Although he got off to a good start in round one, from that point on it was mostly Baer. 15,000 fans watched the bout at Seals Stadium. The bout was slowed down by a heavy rain and a wet ring. Both men exchanged punches throughout but Baer landed the crisper and harder blows. In round three Baer drove Risko all around the ring and had him hanging on. Round six saw Johnny holding his own for the first time since the opening round. Then Baer took the play away in round seven and won that round easily.

In round eight Risko rallied one more time as he pounded Baer both to the head and body. The rain increased in round nine and both men slipped several times. Risko tried his best in round ten but it was too little too late. A few days after the fight it was announced that Baer's $5,000 purse was being held up because of a squabble between Max and his manager, Ham Lorimer. Each claimed the other owed him money.

Back to Cleveland for Dunn and his "Big Fella" for yet another match with the balding K.O. Christner from Akron. The previous fights included a lot of dirty work by both men. Leading up to the November 30, 1931 bout, Risko's manager, Danny Dunn and Christner's manager, Suey Welch, got an agreement with the boxing commission that the upcoming bout would not be terminated by a foul. The referee was going to be instructed to allow both men to heel, cuff and butt, if they were so inclined. The bout was held at Public Hall and turned out to be a very rough fight. In the end Risko had won every round according to the fight report the next day in the Cleveland Plain Dealer. On December 2, 1931, local scribe, Sam Otis, Cleveland Plain Dealer Sports Editor, wrote an editorial titled "No More of Such Stuff". Below the title was the statement "Risko-Christner Bout Proves Boxing Cannot Be Hippodromed in Modern Wrestling Style".

Max Baer gets the nod versus Risko

(San Francisco - November 9, 1931)

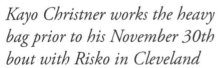

Kayo Christner works the heavy bag prior to his November 30th bout with Risko in Cleveland

As 1932 arrived Risko found himself with several situations that slowed his career to a standstill at times. Risko had a return match all set with Babe Hunt for January 28, 1932, in Miami. It was called off on January 18th because Johnny had hurt his hand playing handball. Promoter Tommy McGinty lost a $2,000 deposit to the city for the cancellation. City law Director W.G. Kerr, told McGinty the money was for rental, ring "set-up", etc. The bout had been scheduled twice, and canceled twice, the last time by the Walker camp.

Meanwhile, manager Dunn was trying to line up fights for Risko not only with Mickey Walker, but also Young Stribling, and even against a come-back for Jack Dempsey. Risko was offered $3,000 to box Jack Dempsey in Cleveland in a four round bout. Risko turned down the offer, insisting that he would only fight the former champ in a normal 10-round contest.

These hit and misses stalled Risko's career and for the first five months of 1932, he did not have a single fight. It was a shame because according to local boxing writer, the highly respected James E. Doyle, of the Cleveland Plain Dealer, as of January 1932, considered Risko a top-ten contender. On January 24, he listed his rankings for the heavyweights as follows: 1. Max Schmeling, 2. Jack Sharkey, 3. Ernie Schaaf, 4. Mickey Walker, 5. Steve Hamas, 6. W.L. Stribling, 7. Primo Carnera, 8. Johnny Risko, 9. King Levinsky, 10. Salvatore Ruggirello.

1932 was certainly off to a rough start. Bouts were tentatively scheduled, then postponed. Wrestling matches were offered to Risko, as well as all sorts of other activities and gimmicks, but not an actual fight. Months went by and the frustration grew and grew. Finally after being postponed at least three times and rescheduled several other times, Johnny was set to meet his twice conqueror, Mickey Walker on June 24th at Cleveland Municipal Stadium.

    Mickey Walker had many friends in the fight business and also in Hollywood. One of them, the famous, sometimes infamous actor, Fatty Arbuckle came to town just prior to Mickey's match with Risko. On the Cleveland-Buffalo train Arbuckle and his fiancee, actress, Addie McPhail, were married when the train made a stop in Wickcliffe, Ohio. Walker attended the wedding. Arbuckle and Miss McPhail were appearing at the RKO Palace Theater in Cleveland during the week of the Risko-Walker fight.

Going into the fight Mickey Walker was favored to win. He was part of the heavyweight title picture and felt that his previous two wins over Risko gave him all the edge he needed. Johnny Risko had his reputation as a spoiler for a good reason, he did it many times in his career. According to the report in the Plain Dealer the next day Risko won seven out of the twelve rounds easily. 15,000 fans saw Johnny win. He started the bout off quickly, almost flooring Walker with a right hand in the second round. In his column the next day in the Cleveland Plain Dealer boxing writer, James E. Doyle stated that "Ragin', rushin' back to the front flight of the heavyweight cauliflorists came old Johnny Risko again last night, with some 15,000 fans howling like all-get-out for him as he steamed through to glorious decision win over brave Mickey Walker at the Cleveland Stadium." (Cleveland Plain Dealer 6-25-32)

Johnny Risko in spite of what Walker's manager Doc Kearns said, won the fight without question. However the battle did not end there. Danny Dunn, manager of Risko, claimed that they got gypped when there was a discrepancy in the figures the Cleveland Boxing Commission listed for attendance and gross receipts and what was reported to the Federal Tax Bureau. This meant according to Dunn that their cut (meaning he and Risko) of the gate was far less than it should have been. Doc Kearns, manager of Walker and the promoter, Tommy McGinty also said they did not understand the figures listed for the fight and felt it needed looked into. On June 27, 1932, there was a story in the Cleveland Plain Dealer telling of a probe being made by the Boxing Commission to determine if there was any merit to Dunn's claim. On June 28th James E. Doyle had a follow-up story in the *Cleveland Plain Dealer.* The headline read:

"After the investigation the fight crowd was listed as 14,579 and the Gate $16,269.75."

The story went on to say that the officials listed 698 as Annie Oakley customers, meaning they had passes. However Commissioner Paul Hoynes told the writer, "We don't know how many weren't accounted for. It might have been two and it might have been 2,000."

Eddie Mead, working as first lieutenant to Mr. Tommy McGinty, the promoter claimed there weren't enough ticket takers to handle the crowd and that is why people got tired of waiting and crashed. (Cleveland Plain Dealer 6-28-32)

The bottom line is although many of the parties involved felt there was something not right with the payout, even after the investigation it remained a mystery.

On June 29, 1932, the great writer Grantland Rice wrote a piece in the *Cleveland Plain Dealer* praising Risko's win over Walker. It appeared below as shown:

"Amazing Risko

The point has been made that Max Schmeling should now meet the outstanding challenger before facing Sharkey in a return match. The next point is this - Who is the outstanding challenger?

Ernie Schaaf, Mickey Walker and Primo Carnera have all been thumped around lately, and they were supposed to be the top column of the challenging division. So there are no outstandees in sight.

The amazing Johnny Risko kept Sharkey out of a Tunney fight four years ago. And long after he was supposed to be through Risko lays a stymie for Mickey Walker and at least removes part of a glitter which a Schmeling-Walker fight might have assumed.

Jack Dempsey may develop something from his Levinksy-Baer battle in Reno next week. At least there is a chance if a knockout or a decisive winning happens to take place. As it is now, there are too many on just about an even basis to work up much froth."

On August 1st, Risko finally got back into action as he met Tuffy Griffith, the contender from Sioux City who had defeated him three times, twice by decision and once by a foul. The fight was held at Cleveland Municipal Stadium and 10,146 fans showed up to watch Johnny pound out a twelve-round decision. The fight report appeared as shown below in the *Cleveland Plain Dealer*.

"Fight By Rounds

ROUND 1 -They sparred in the center of the ring. Risko hooked a left to the stomach. Griffith drove a left to Johnny's belt line. Griffith crossed a hard right to the jaw and followed with a harder right to the ear. Tuffy blocked a left and they clinched. Griffith missed a vicious right and Risko slammed a left to the body. Griffith popped a right to the chin. Risko put a straight left to the nose. Griffith jabbed a left to the nose. Risko outpunched Griffith in a clinch. Griffith tapped a left and a right to the head and then shot a right to the body. Risko rapped a left and right to the head and then crashed a left to the body. Griffith took a hard right on the head just before the round ended.

ROUND 2- They sparred in the center of the ring. Risko's left went around Tuffy's neck and they clinched. Griffith shot a left to the nose. Risko crashed a hard left and a right to the body and the crowd roared. Risko put a right to the body and a left to the head. Griffith hooked a left to the head. Risko jabbed three lefts to the nose. Risko rushed in with a right to the ribs. As they came out of a clinch, Risko stung Griffith with a right to the chin. Griffith charged, punching to the body and Johnny covered up in a neutral corner. Risko knocked Griffith reeling against the ropes with a left and a right hook to the jaw. Tuffy hung on. After the clinch Risko looped a left to the head. Griffith started for a neutral corner at the bell.

ROUND 3- They sparred in the center of the ring, then clinched. Risko shot a left to the boy which Griffith partly blocked. Griffith was short with a terrific right and they clinched. Risko scored with three left jabs. Griffith left jabbed twice to Risko's face. Risko jabbed two lefts to the chin followed with a left hook to the jaw. Johnny jabbed again and they clinched. Risko hammered a right to the heart. Risko hooked a left to the jaw and they clinched. Griffith dropped a good right on Johnny's jaw. Griffith crossed a right to the chin and Johnny retaliated with a left and right to the body. They clinched at the end of the round.

ROUND 4- After twenty seconds of sparring Griffith shook Risko with a right cross to the chin. Then they clinched. They traded stiff punches near the ropes. Again Griffith crossed a right to the chin and again Risko boxed cautiously for several seconds. Then he put a light right tot he ribs. Risko hooked a left to the ribs and they clinched. Griffith tore in with left and right to the body. Griffith turned Risko around with a right to the jaw. Risko smiled and drove left right to the body. Risko did all the punching in a clinch. Griffith shook Johnny with another hard right to the jaw. They were coming out of a clinch as the bell rang.

ROUND 5- Risko shot a left to the jaw and Griffith cracked a better left to the body. Griffith jabbed three lefts to the mouth. Griffith hooked a left to the stomach. Risko rushed in with a right to the ribs and they clinched. Risko jabbed a left to the mouth and Griffith a left to the ribs. They punched evenly in the center of the ring. Risko drove Griffith to the ropes with a left hook to the jaw and then came in with a right hook to the stomach. Griffith hooked a left to the stomach. Risko was low with a left hook and Griffith winced. Risko jabbed a left to the nose. Risko's left went over Griffith's head and they clinched. Risko crashed a right in the heart and then hooked left and right to the jaw. Once more Griffith started for the wrong corner after the bell.

ROUND 6- They sparred and Griffith crossed a hard right to the jaw. Griffith crossed a hard right to the jaw. Griffith hooked a left to the body and they clinched. Risko outpunched Griffith in another clinch. As Risko missed with a right, Griffith brought up a jarring right to Johnny's chin. Griffith advanced swinging left and right and Johnny covered up momentarily. Griffith outscored Johnny in an exchange at close quarters. Risko hooked a left to the stomach and brought up a right that glanced off Tuffy's chin. Griffith missed with a right and they clinched. Griffith jabbed a left to the mouth and Johnny sent a left to the body. Griffith hooked a left to the jaw at the bell.

ROUND 7- They sparred under the center light. Risko hooked good left and right to the body. Griffith drove a right to the ribs. Risko hooked a sweeping left to the jaw and then outpunched Tuffy in a clinch. Now left and right to the body drove Griffith back. Risko landed a right to the ribs in a clinch. Griffith jabbed a left to the nose and they clinched again. Risko drove a right to the heart and followed with a hard left to the stomach. Again the right reached Griffith's heart. Near the ropes Johnny registered with a right to the heart for a third time. They traded wallops in the center of the ring and as Griffith broke away Johnny brought up a right uppercut to the chin. Griffith jabbed a left to the mouth. They were sparring at the bell.

ROUND 8- They went into a clinch as Griffith missed with a right. Risko scored with a left and right to the body. Risko did most of the punching in a clinch. Griffith crossed a stiff right to the chin. Another right to the jaw shook Johnny. Twice Griffith charged and twice they clinched. Griffith volleyed left and right to the stomach. A right reached Risko's ear. Griffith shot two rights to the jaw and Johnny covered up as they backed to the ropes. They punched evenly in the center of the ring. Risko jabbed a left to the mouth and they clinched. Griffith's right landed on Johnny's head. They were clinched. Risko punching his right to the ribs as the round ended.

ROUND 9- They sparred and then Griffith scored a good right to the chin. Risko missed with a left and they clinched. Griffith outpunched Johnny in another clinch near the ropes. They clinched once more, each punching to the body. Griffith shot two rights to the head and Risko hooked a left to the body. Griffith hooked a left to the chin as Johnny was dancing away. Risko hooked a left to the chin. Griffith crossed a right to the ear. They traded left jabs after a clinch. Risko jabbed a left to the mouth and Griffith jabbed a left to the chin. Risko missed with a left as they clinched. Griffith's right glanced off Johnny's head as the bell rang.

ROUND 10- Griffith hooked a left to the stomach and they clinched. They sparred and clinched again. Risko jabbed a left to the body. The action was slowing up temporarily. They clinched and Griffith put a left to the ribs. Risko was short with a left and they clinched again. They punched evenly at close range, each shooting for the body. Risko jabbed a left to the nose and they clinched. Risko cut looose (sic) with a left and with a left and right to the body, forcing Griffith to the ropes. Risko jabbed a left to the chin and hooked a right to the heart. Risko landed two lefts to the nose and raised Griffith's head with a right uppercut to the chin. Griffith missed with a right and Risko hooked a left to the pit of the stomach at the bell.

ROUND 11- Griffith tapped a left to the jaw and they clinched. Risko outpunched Griffith in another clinch. Griffith hooked a light left to the jaw. They clinched and then sparred. Riskio had the edge in the close-up exchange. Griffith's right bounced off Risko's head. Risko hooked right and left to the stomach. Griffith crossed a right to the jaw. Risko came in with a right to the stomach. Risko jabbed a left to the nose and again plastered a right to the stomach. Risko took a right on the jaw and then shook Tuffy with a right to the jaw and left to the stomach. Griffith put left and right to the stomach. They were punching in mid-ring at the gong.

ROUND 12- Griffith jabbed a left to the nose and they clinched. Each punched to the body in another clinch. Risko jabbed a left to the mouth. Risko jabbed a left to the nose and hooked a left to the body. Up close Risko hooked a left to the body and brought up a short right to the jaw. Griffith jabbed a left to the face and they clinched. Griffith hooked a left to the stomach and they clinched. Griffith was wild with a right. They traded hard punches to the body. Risko had the advantage as they slugged near the ropes. Johnny drove Tuffy in a neutral corner. Punching to the body and the crowd howled. Griffith hung on. They were punching at the bell. "

Things were looking up for Johnny Risko in 1932. After his two big wins over Walker and Griffith an article appeared in the Boston Globe on August 3 where Jack Sharkey was quoted in the headline:

"BRING ON RISKO SAYS SHARKEY".

Madison Square Garden held the exclusive rights to promoting Sharkey's fights. They were more than willing to grant the heavyweight champion's wishes. Cleveland Plain Dealer writer James E. Doyle, on August 4th, questioned whether Jack Sharkey really meant it. He wondered if the Boston Gob really was willing to take on Risko again. Although Sharkey maintained he was robbed in his 1928 bout with Risko in New York, the fact remained that Risko won nine rounds on most scorecards. Doyle's suspicions seemed valid because on August 15th the former heavyweight champion, Max Schmeling was signed to meet Mickey Walker in a fifteen-round fight in Madison Square Garden. The bout, was set for September 19th . The winner was said to battle with the champion Sharkey for the title. The headline in New York read:

"RISKO IGNORED IN SPITE OF BIG COMEBACK."

On August 23, 1932, local writer Alex Zirin wrote that Risko's recent victories were not in vain and that if he got by King Levinsky on September 1st in Cleveland, that he was in line to get a return match with Max Schmeling. The German was the only opponent who ever was able to stop the Rubber Man and that was of the technical variety. This was just the opposite of what was being written in New York.

Meanwhile the September 1st Cleveland bout with King Levinsky went off as scheduled at Cleveland Stadium. This was part of the Cleveland News Christmas fund show. As he had in their previous bout the year before in Boston, Risko outboxed the Kingfish to gain the twelve round decision. Risko used his left jab to pile up points. He won eight rounds easily and the hardest blows Levinsky landed were south of the border. In the fourth, eighth, ninth, tenth and eleventh rounds Levinsky was warned by referee, Matt Brock to bring his punches up. Although the fans booed at times and the fight was not as exciting as the Walker and Griffith matches in June and August, the 10,504 fans were treated to an entertaining fight overall.

—30-year old Johnny Risko was not going to have too many more opportunities to land a title shot.

After the Levinsky win, Madision Square Garden was said to be seeking a Risko-Max Baer match. Johnny was on vacation and other offers were pouring in. Supposedly Chicago was seeking a Risko-Carnera match and Omaha promoters were looking to lock up a Risko-Dick Daniels rematch. Danny Dunn felt Johnny deserved a rest, that he had not ever trained as hard as he had for his last three matches.

On September 20, 1932, the N.B.A (National Boxing Association) announced in a Baltimore headline: Risko Wins No. 4 Rating as Heavyweight Contender. The ratings were by the NBA (National Boxing Association) and after champion, Jack Sharkey, were Max Schmeling, Max Baer, Stanley Poreda, and then Johnny Risko.

It would seem that Johnny Risko was sitting pretty. But no other fights were lined up as the last three months of 1932 went by. Once again Risko's career was filled with uncertainty. In this writer's opinion if anyone deserved a title shot at this time it was Johnny Risko!

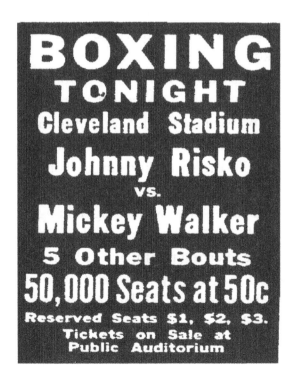

The Last Hurrah 1933-34

As 1932 ended it appeared Johnny Risko was finally on the verge of a title shot. He had revitalized his career with some important wins and was ranked in the top five of the heavyweight division. It would seem every other week the sports fans would pick up a newspaper and see another proposed fight for Risko

In early January of 1933, local promoter Tommy McGinty, who had national connections, was trying to tie down a third match between Max Baer and Risko in Miami Beach, Florida for late January or February. It didn't happen.

Meanwhile the inactivity dragged on for Johnny. In the January 10th Cleveland Plain Dealer Risko posed in a derby hat and fancy coat with a cigar hanging out of his mouth. The title of the article was: Risko as You Seldom See Him. They were referring to him as a fashion-plate. The story also mentioned that Johnny weighed 220 pounds, far above his normal fighting weight. His lack of action was apparently catching up with him.

On February 5, 1933, the Cleveland Plain Dealer's Jame E. Doyle wrote that "Risko signed for Coliseum bout; Simms sought as a foe". Local promoter Walter Taylor was looking forward to matching up Risko with another local heavyweight, Eddie Simms, at the East 46th & Euclid Avenue venue. It never came off.

Finally in the February 7th *Cleveland Plain Dealer* it was announced that Johnny Risko and King Levinsky were once again matched, this time in New York. Johnny looked to make it three in a row over the fish peddler. According to Danny Dunn, promoter Walter Taylor had agreed to postpone the Coliseum match so Risko could fight Levinsky in Madison Square Garden. Although Risko had not fought since the September meeting with Levinsky, the Kingfish had fought twice, defeating Unknown Winston by decision at Philadelphia and then knocking out K.O. Christner at St. Nicholas rink in New York. Still the "Diminutive" Danny Dunn felt optimistic that a big win over Levinsky "Is a great chance for us to break into the big dough all over again. If John can turn in one of his sensational fights against Levinsky, the kind he's usually put up in New York, who knows who we will get as the winner."

Even though he was up two wins to none over Levinsky, Risko found himself on the short end of 8-5 odds going into the Levinsky match. Their fight had been postponed out of deference to Ernie Schaaf's memory. Schaaf had died after his February 10th match with huge Primo Carnera. He had taken a bad beating from Max Baer prior to that meeting.

Risko and Dunn had been trying to get a match with Primo Carnera, feeling Risko would take the "Ambling Alp". But first he had to defeat Levinsky. Odds or no odds when Risko and Levinsky met for the third time on February 24, 1933, the end result was the same, Risko won the decision.

The New York headlines read Risko's Wild Rushes Beat Back Levinsky. 10,000 fans saw Johnny give Levinsky a thorough trouncing in their ten round fight. It was called by reporter, Edward Neil, "A fine old Pier 6 brawl between a couple of the roughest warriors in the ring today." Risko staggered Levinsky several times. The Associated Press at the end gave Risko six rounds, Levinsky three, with one even. Risko was in fine shape for this fight, weighing 199$^{1/2}$ to Levinsky's 196. At times he actually danced around the Kingfish throwing out stinging jabs and seemed in control throughout. When the action got hot and heavy the referee, Pete Hartley, half the size of both men, had a hard time trying to pry the combatants apart at the bell and needed the assistance of the corner men. The scoring of the fight was odd at best. Most everyone felt Cleveland's Rubber Man won the fight. Referee Hartley and one judge voted for Johnny but the other judge cast his vote for the Chicago fish peddler. This made five impressive wins in a row for Risko.

On February 27th the great Grantland Rice wrote a nice story on Risko in the *Cleveland Plain Dealer*. He remarked about the ups and downs of Risko's career and how he had spoiled the best laid plans of Tex Rickard by defeating his hand picked contenders. Rice commented that Risko not only met all the good fighters in the last eight years but he met most of them two or three times. In one particular paragraph he really summed it up when he said:

"Max Schmeling alone has knocked him out and that knockout was supposed to be Risko's closing chapter. Yet many years later, the chunky Cleveland boy is winning decisions from young fighters rated along the top row, with no particular sign of fading out. He has been one of the most durable heavyweights ever known...a trial horse with the epidermis of a rhinoceros. Risko has won no championship, but he has barred the championship road to more than a few."

On March 1, 1933, Johnny appeared in a *Cleveland Plain Dealer* article but not for a fight announcement but rather because an incident involving his father, John Risko Sr., age 54. Apparently the senior Risko was involved in a disturbance but not under the proper circumstances. John's father was a guest at the County Jail in Elyria, Ohio, pending a payment of a fine of $30.00 and costs, assessed by Mayor Edward Burrell of Sheffield Lake Village, Ohio. Johnny was quoted as saying he would pay the fine after his father "learned his lesson." (Cleveland Plain Dealer 3-1-33)

On March 5th is was reported that Risko signed to meet Mickey Walker once again in New York, on either March 24th or the 31st. Johnny was confident he would knock out the Toy Bulldog this time. But on March 12th the fight was postponed because of a financial situation at Madison Square Garden that wasn't revealed. Risko and Walker would never again meet in the ring.

On March 28, 1933, Risko met Dick Daniels for a second time at the Coliseum at East 46th and Euclid Avenue in Cleveland. This bout proved to be bad for Johnny in more ways than one. In the very first round Daniels launched an attack that had Risko on the deck twice. Later it was revealed that Johnny badly damaged his right ankle during one of the knockdowns. It turned out to be far worse than anyone probably could have imagined at the time. Risko not only continued on with the fight but actually had Daniels on the verge of a knockout two rounds later. If the bell hadn't sounded to end the third round, the record books would have shown Risko KO3. But the bell did ring and saved Daniels. Johnny traveled the last nine rounds on his bum ankle and showed great courage even if he did lose the decision. Ironically Daniels cut of the gate was a mere $348.16 and Risko received $812.37. X-rays later revealed that Johnny had torn tendons, and it put him on crutches and out of commission for almost three months.

Manager Danny Dunn, never short of wisecracks, commented to Johnny after the fight:

"Well, that's about as much as a fella kin expect when he goes jay-walkin."

"Wa'd'ya mean...jaywalking?" asked Johnny.

"Why, what else do you do? Walkin' out there and stickin' yer chin in the the way o' that mugg's Western Union right! Invited it, didn'tcha?"

Cleveland Plain Dealer (4-3-33)

The ankle injury apparently killed any last chance of another Walker match. Meanwhile with Risko on the shelf local heavyweights Eddie Simms and Patsy Perroni were matched in an eight-round bout on the card featuring Gorilla Jones and Ben Jeby, at Public Hall on April 19, 1933. Perroni was riding a seventeen bout winning streak. It was the first time in years local fight fans had plenty to talk about that did not include Johnny Risko in the conversation. The two youngsters had plenty of fans. Perroni won an easy decision over Simms and hoped to meet Risko when his ankle healed.

Leading up to the match the *Cleveland Plain Dealer* on June 12, 1933, called the proposed match between Risko and Perroni:

"HEAVY "NATURAL" STIRS LOCAL FANS.
Risko-Perroni Bout Is First Big All-Cleveland Class Since 1924."

Finally on June 20, 1933, Johnny Risko was ready to meet Patsy Perroni at Public Hall. Originally scheduled for Cleveland Stadium, the weather caused two postponements. Risko's manager, Danny Dunn originally had agreed to a $4,000 purse with promoter Harry Cohen. But leading up to the fight Dunn suddenly asked Cohen for a $7,500 guarantee. Cohen said, "I guess Johnny doesn't want to fight Perroni." Apparently the parties involved came up with a meeting of the minds because the bout finally came off. Risko was nine years older than the Canton, Ohio youngster and weighed fourteen pounds more, otherwise their size was mostly equal. Perroni was considered a skillful boxer and fine puncher. His biggest wins leading to the Risko fight were decision victories over the previously undefeated Adolf Heuser and distance wins over Joe Sekyra and Tom Heeney.

The report in the *Cleveland Plain Dealer* on June 21st, by James E. Doyle said it all:

"PERRONI WINS SEVEN ROUNDS TO WHIP RISKO."

The youngster from Canton, Ohio, Perroni started the fight quickly and appeared too fast for the Rubber Man. He landed stinging lefts and hard rights throughout the fight. 6,350 fans surely must have felt they were watching the changing of the guard as Patsy landed left hooks and right crosses consistently during most every round. Risko staggered and came back for more but he could not match Perroni's amount of work and was well beaten at the end. However as usual in most if not all of Risko's fights, Johnny never showed quit in him. In the ten and final round Risko landed a wicked left hook to the chops of Perroni that buckled his knees and almost floored him. At the end, however it was just a matter of announcing the decision that everyone knew was coming. Patsy Perroni had scored his biggest win to date. Meanwhile Primo Carnera won the heavyweight title with a 6th round kayo over Jack Sharkey, in Long Island City, New York, on June 29, 1933. A very suspicious fight in the view of many experts.

A month later on July 26, 1933, Johnny went to Chicago to once again meet Tommy Loughran, the former light-heavy champ. Loughran was trying to work his way back into the heavyweight title picture, but he found out that Risko's role as a spoiler had not yet ended. Appearing in excellent condition Risko charged out of his corner and launched a two-fisted body attack that appeared to bewilder the former light-heavyweight champion. Johnny launched a left hook to the chin that just missed but then he shot up a right uppercut that landed flush and Loughran spilled over and half way through the ropes. Tommy was hurt but somehow weathered the storm to survive the round. In the second and third rounds Loughran found the range and boxed nicely to win both of those rounds. In the fourth Risko renewed his aggressive attack and continued the assault in the fifth and sixth rounds. Loughran had the edge in the seventh round but from the eighth round on Risko kept forcing the action and piled up points to his margin. At the end Risko was the winner of yet another comeback. On July 31, 1933, Grantland Rice wrote a nice piece on the exploits of Johnny Risko again in The Cleveland Plain Dealer. It read as follows:

"Risko - Tester and Wrecker

When it comes to worth as a combined tester and wrecker of championship hopes, the main award must go to Johnny Risko, the Cleveland Rubber Man.

As a starter, Risko came near checking Tunney's dream before Tunney met Dempsey. Tunney won the twelve-round battle, but he had a hard fight, and Risko was in there swinging lustily at the finish. Not knowing how good Risko was, many began to mutter about Tunney's chances in a Dempsey show.

Later on, when Tunney was on top, Tex Rickard had practically named Jack Sharkey as the leading challenger. But Sharkey had one elimination to meet and Risko seemed to be the leading choice. At the that time Sharkey was confident that Risko couldn't win a round. Rickard felt almost as strongly in the matter.

But when the war opened Risko jumped out to win seven of the first eight rounds and then romp away with the decision by a half dozen kilometers.

He almost spoiled Tom Heeney's chance. Also Paulino's outlook. In fact, he was scrambling Rickard's programs month after month.

Tex figured that Risko cost him close to a half million dollars by outmauling one prospective champ after another, including Paul Berlenbach, who was then at his peak.

A short while ago Mickey Walker decided on a comeback campaign. He ran into Johnny Risko and bounded back out of the picture.

Then Tommy Loughran gets going at something like his old speed. He is on his way in a hurry - until he hits Risko. And Tommy's dream of a heavyweight march is practically over. This makes about eight years in which the famous Rubber Man has been jabbing a long pin into the balloons of ambitious fighters.

Being of the "can take it" breed, he was supposed to be walking on his heels by now. But he keeps on walking forward when the battle is on, whether upon heels or toes.

The Rubber boy is still able to bounce. No one yet has been able to remove his remarkable elasticity, or discourage him from taking his wind-up."

Johnny Risko was not only highly regarded by some of the best sports writers of the time, he was usually well thought of by former opponents. In the August 15, 1933, Cleveland Plain Dealer appeared a column called They Say -- In addition to several quotes by local and international politicians and clergy were a couple by former and current boxers. Max Baer (asked if he got a "kick" out of seeing movie stars) said, "Not any more. I pass them and they look at me." But what was more interesting to Cleveland fight fans was the last quote in the column. Former heavyweight champ Gene Tunney stated "Johnny Risko was the toughest man I ever fought."

Johnny Risko was often generous with his time and offered to help various charity groups in the Cleveland area. On September 18, 1933, he was involved with a "Boxing For Milk Fund" show that was to raise funds to provide milk for undernourished pupils of public and parochial schools of East Cleveland. The program involved six boxing and wrestling matches, all amateur, which were refereed by sports celebrities including Johnny Risko.

On October 27th Johnny Risko almost lost his trainer and conditioner, Freddy Rogers, to a fluke accident. Rogers who did not travel with Danny Dunn and Johnny to Texas for a series of upcoming bouts went to the gymnasium at 1421 Castle Avenue to open it up. An American Bulldog named Mike followed the trainer inside. The dog was the property of Danny Dunn. Rogers lit a fire in a gas stove in the office as Mike sprawled in front of the stove. While Rogers was sitting down to read some mail from Dunn he suddenly felt sleepy and couldn't keep his head up. The next thing he knew Rogers felt Mike biting him on the hand and dragging him to his feet. Then the dog caught hold of Freddy's trouser leg and tugged him across the room to the door. Rogers noticed as he stumbled across the office floor that the fire in the stove had gone out and that gas was hissing from the burner, "Mike saved my life, Rogers said." (*Cleveland Plain Dealer 10-28-33*)

On October 30, 1933, Risko finally got back into action as he met Big Boy Peterson in Houston, Tex and stopped him in the 6th round after having him on the floor six different times. The final blow was a left to the body. Risko weighing 210 pounds, had a six pound weight advantage. Peterson was a trial horse at best and retired after the Risko loss.

Risko had a second bout in Texas, this time in Dallas on November 9th, against Jack Van Noy. Van Noy was a former football star from The University of Oklahoma and was based out of Los Angeles. Van Noy, like Risko's previous opponent Big Boy Peterson, was not a very good fighter. But at the end of the fight he was awarded the 10-round decision. According to the local papers Risko won the first five rounds handily and even though Van Noy landed some hard blows in the middle rounds, Risko was punishing him throughout and at the end of the bout Van Noy's mid-section was red from the pounding. Yet one judge voted for Risko, one for Van Noy and the referee gave the nod to the Los Angeles fighter. Risko's stablemate, Gene Stanton forwarded a clipping from the Dallas News, to Cleveland Plain Dealer boxing writer, James E. Doyle. Doyle printed it as it appears in his column in the November 14, 1933 *Cleveland Plain Dealer*.

"A Texan Tells It.
Johnny Risko spoiler of heavyweight championship aspirants, can vouch for the fact that Texas is in the embryo

stage with something to learn as far as boxing is concerned. Or maybe it is Johnny who learned something about risking his reputation in the fistic wildernesses. For after pounding Jack I'an Roy all over the ring he saw his opponents hand raised in token of victory.

According to the News' scorecard, Risko made an easy sweep of the first five rounds. He also won the eighth and ninth, with the seventh even and the sixth and tenth going to I' an Noy, Jack grabbing the final heat because John was obviously coasting.

Risko forced most of the fighting, kept Jack back-pedaling, feinted him open to one sucker punch after another and jarred him with looping blows to the head."

Even though he officially lost the bout to Van Noy, when the N.B.A. (National Boxing Association) came out with their ratings of heavyweights on December 19, 1933, Johnny Risko was still listed as the sixth best heavyweight in the world behind champion Primo Carnera, Max Baer, Max Schmeling, Tommy Loughran and King Levinsky. Even with that high ranking it seemed odd that Loughran and Levinsky were ahead of Risko. Still as 1934 quickly approached there seemed to be hope.

Boxing has always had sad stories about fighters who hung around too long, took too much punishment, or ended up broke. An article in the paper on January 9, 1934, told of former light-heavy champ, Paul Berlenbach appearing as a wrestler at Madison Square Garden. The story also mentioned the fact that John Risko had derailed Paul's ambitions to be the heavyweight champion back in 1926, when he soundly whipped him. Also on January 9th Risko met up again with old foe Jimmy Maloney of Boston, this time in Miami, Florida. Cleveland's favorite spoiler once again played his favorite role as he won an easy decision over Maloney and ruined his comeback. Maloney had scored three straight victories before meeting up with Johnny again. Risko scored two knockdowns in the fourth round. The bell saved Maloney after the second one. Risko was awarded all ten rounds when the decision was announced.

Cleveland Plain Dealer

After the Maloney victory Danny Dunn still was talking about Johnny meeting Primo Carnera. He had tried to match him with the giant Italian earlier on but because the fight had to be "on the up and up", Carnera's management wanted no part of the Rubber Man. Ironically Risko and Carnera flew together down to Macon, Georgia on March 4th to attend a memorial boxing exhibition to be given in honor of the late Young Stribling, who had tragically died in a motorcycle accident on October 3, 1933, at the age of 28. Primo boxed an exhibition with an unnamed fighter. Johnny Risko and light heavyweight champion, Maxie Rosenbloom clowned through four rounds.

Promoter Lew Diamond signed Risko to fight former light-heavyweight champion, Bob Godwin at Daytona Beach Florida on February 28, 1934. The fight got postponed but finally came off on March 22nd. Godwin had briefly held the light-heavy title but lost it after just two months in 1933. Spotting Risko 18 1/2 pounds he pounded out a decisive decision after ten rounds. He kept hammering Risko with a series of left jabs and straight right hands. Although there were no knockdowns Risko stumbled to the wrong corner after the third round. Johnny threw plenty of blows but couldn't seem to land on Godwin who continued to dance and weave throughout the fight.

As had been the norm during this time, several bouts were proposed for Risko that never came off. Larry Atkins, who had taken over for Tommy McGinty as matchmaker tried to land Steve Hamas or Tommy Loughran as opponents for Risko. He failed to land either of them.

Rumors started to spread that Risko had hung up his gloves. They proved to be false and on May 22, 1934, Risko went back into training full time. A proposed fight with Natie Brown was in the works. Risko was quoted as saying he was off the sweets he loved so much and would still love to meet Max Schmeling again, or Primo Carnera or Max Baer. When asked if he was still sore about not getting a second shot at Schmeling his response was, "He's a tramp, but I'd like to show him my own self. Carnera is a tramp too. I saw that when I watched him with poor old Tommy Loughran at Florida."

Finally on June 4, 1934, Risko was matched up with Natie Brown in Washington D.C. Brown had once been a sparring partner for Max Schmeling and supposedly was let go because he hit too hard. A crowd of 15,000 watched Brown get off to a quick start and build up a big lead with a rapier left hand. Brown took advantage of Risko's slow start to repeatedly knock the Clevelander off balance. Risko had entered the ring with a cut over his left eye and Brown opened the wound quickly. Risko tried to rally in the late rounds but the fight was out of hand by then. However although the fight appeared to be all Brown's, when the votes were taken Referee Howard Livingstone and Judge Frank Schuyler voted for Brown; but Judge Buck Greer cast his ballot for Risko. The fight was the first ever held in Griffith's Stadium.

Eddie Mead who had managed many fighters, including Cleveland's Paul Pirrone, also promoted from time to time. Once again he tried to match up Risko with fellow Clevelander, Eddie Simms. Mead claimed he had Simms under contract but that Risko had not shown any willingness to mix it up with the Slovenian. According to a local editorial on June 8, 1934, Simms was "So eager to meet Risko that yesterday he offered to turn over his entire purse to charity if he didn't succeed in whipping Johnny, if and- when-they meet." —*Cleveland Plain Dealer* (6-8-34)

When asked on June 13, 1934, who he thought would win the Carnera-Baer fight, Risko responded in the Cleveland Plain Dealer: "Baer almost broke his right hand on my jaw the night I beat him," says Johnny Risko, "and he didn't know what t' make of it when I asked him t' stop ticklin'. Thought I was kiddin', he did, and I was never more serious in my life. "But this big Eyetalian won't think HE's gettin' tickled. When he wakes up he'll be askin' if anybody got the number o' the truck that hit him." —*Cleveland Plain Dealer* (6-13-34)

On June 14, 1934, Max Baer won the heavyweight championship with an 11th round technical knockout over Primo Carnera. Baer had the Italian down at least eleven times and played with him throughout the bout. It was no contest. I doubt anyone thought it would be if they had followed the career of Carnera. Referee Arthur Donovan mercifully stopped the contest to prevent Carnera from further punishment.

Besides not getting matched up with Eddie Simms, nor Jack Sharkey, Max Schmeling or Max Baer again, another former opponent Johnny was not going to meet again was Dick Daniels. The Minnesota heavyweight who claimed two victories over Johnny found himself sentenced to five years in the state reformatory on June 25, 1934. He was found guilty of the theft of six fur coats from a fur store.

On July 24, 1934, Risko got a return match with upstart, Patsy Perroni, at Public Hall. 6,632 fans saw Perroni once again win the 10-round decision. Johnny started fast and won the first three rounds with his aggressive attack of looping lefts and rights, forcing Perroni to the ropes several times. Perroni withstood the attack, however, and rallied in the fourth round, pounding lefts and rights to Risko's body. Risko got staggered in the seventh, ninth and tenth rounds. The late rally apparently won the fight for Perroni. The Cleveland Plain Dealer reported on July 25th that the unanimous verdict for Perroni was loudly booed.

On August 8th Johnny met former light-heavyweight champion, Tommy Loughran for the fifth and last time in his career. The bout was held in Freeport, Long Island, New York. Johnny pounded out a ten-round decision that was well received by the 7,000 fans on hand. Risko's aggressiveness once again won the fight for him. Loughran, the boxing master tried to keep Risko at bay with his long left but Johnny keep moving inside. His indifference to punishment aided by his wicked body shots, were more than enough to earn the unanimous decision for the Cleveland Rubber Man. In the eighth round Loughran caught Risko with a perfectly time right cross to the jaw as he was coming in and nearly floored him.

As usual Risko quickly recovered and was exchanging blows with Loughran as the round ended. The weights were 182 3/4 pounds for Loughran to 195 for Risko. The bout was staged for the benefit of the Holy Redeemer School of Freeport.

Johnny Risko: The Cleveland Rubber Man

Risko's next bout had a weird ending. On August 18, 1934, Risko went to Green Bay, Wisconsin to meet Adolph Wiater. The weather did not cooperate and neither did Wiater as he had Johnny on the defensive during the first four rounds. Rain came in a steady downpour just as the fifth round was to start and Referee Walter Houleman stopped the fight. Risko had three stitches taken in a cut on his lip after the fight. The promoters tried to reschedule the fight but for some reason it never happened. It appears in Risko's record as a No Contest 5.

The third match-up between Johnny Risko and Patsy Perroni occurred on December 10, 1934, at Public Hall. The Canton, Ohio native made it 3-0 as he won another decision over the gallant Risko. This time is was a split-decision with the two judges, Herb Williams and Al Porter voting for Perroni and the referee, Matt Brock casting his ballot for Risko. There were times during the match that Johnny landed two or three blows to one on Perroni but the Italian's punches appeared to carry much more authority. Risko did force the action most of the time. His left hook was working with frequency and to some, including referee Brock, he did enough to win the fight. At the end Risko was disconsolate and felt he was gypped of the decision.

1934 was coming to a close but Danny Dunn and Johnny Risko continued on their quest to get back into heavyweight contention one last time.

On December 19th Johnny met Harry English in Toledo, Ohio. Outweighing English by ten pounds, he had no trouble winning the decision. English came out punching and was taking it to Risko in the second round when Risko floored him with a left hook. He barely got up at nine and managed to survive the round. The fight show was a Christmas charity card, something with which Johnny always managed to be involved.

On December 28, 1934, Risko finished out the year with yet another controversial decision loss. He met Charley Retzlaff at Minneapolis before a large crowd and he appeared to have the upper hand in most of the rounds. When the decision was announced for Retzlaff the crowd loudly booed. Little did local fight fans know that the Retzlaff fight would be Johnny's last one for a long time.

Johnny Risko (left) with sparring partner Johnnie Poffek (Miami, Florida 1933).

The Final Fights 1935-40

As they say all good things must come to an end. As 1934 came to an end so basically did Risko's days as a contender. There were several rumors about Johnny fighting up and coming Detroit heavyweight Joe Louis. In the January 6, 1935, Cleveland Plain Dealer a post stated that Johnny Risko was definitely not going to fight Louis. But a week later writer James E. Doyle wrote a column saying that Max Baer and Johnny Risko were being sought by two different promoters. Al Paige and Tommy McGinty both stated they were seeking to match the two up for a third time. Al Paige even conferred with Ancil Hoffman, Baer's manager and related that Mr. Hoffman gave him a large head of encouragement. Risko's main man, Danny Dunn, said it didn't matter to him who promoted the bout as long as Risko could meet Baer again. It never came close to coming off.

In his June 15, 1935, column in the Cleveland Plain Dealer, James E. Doyle spoke of James Braddock winning the heavyweight title. Risko's manager Dunn lamented that

it didn't seem fair that Braddock got a title shot.
"We had t' fight ev'rybody-Tunney, Sharkey, Heeney, Godfrey and all the rest-here's a lucky guy that gets a title shot off two winnin' fights. Off beatin' John Henry Lewis and Art Lasky." —*Cleveland Plain Dealer (6-15-35)*

The rumors about Johnny Risko meeting Joe Louis seem to persist. In the August 2, 1935, *Cleveland Plain Dealer* there was a story saying Mike Jacobs, now the bigwig in New York boxing felt that Risko was still favored to fight Joe Louis in New York and that perhaps it could draw a gate of $200,000. Time went on and no bout was set.

On some record sources it shows Johnny Risko winning a 10-rd decision over a fighter named Jess Calhoun on November 11, 1935, in Louisville. I could not find any report or story on this supposed fight. In addition when I looked up the name Jess Calhoun it indeed showed a fighter by that name but listed him as a lightweight. So, as far as I can tell, Johnny Risko was inactive during 1935.

As late as December 19, 1935, Danny Dunn was still talking about Risko meeting Joe Louis. He claimed Johnny was in excellent shape and training hard for the first time in many months.

Finally on January 3, 1936, it was announced that Risko had lost the Louis fight and Joe Louis was instead going to meet Abe Feldman, at the Olympic Arena in Detroit, Michigan. Johnny Risko who had been the promoters first choice as a prospective opponent for Joe Louis, left Cleveland a week before. "John thought they were giving him the old runaround," said Manager Danny Dunn. "I knew that

Johnny Risko: The Cleveland Rubber Man

they weren't, but I couldn't convince him. Then when I told 'em he'd gone to Florida, they picked Feldman."

Risko was one of the reasons the fight game enjoyed a resurgence in Cleveland.

Also in January of 1936, Paul Risko, Johnny's younger brother entered the local Golden Gloves in the Novice Division as a middleweight. His only resemblance to Johnny was that Paul could take a lot of punishment. He won a wild slugging match against his first opponent Emil Beneclik. In his next fight he got knocked down in the last round and was eliminated by decision against Sal Silkoff. Paul was a gifted musician and orchestra leader. He resembled Johnny in appearance but didn't have his fighting ability.

On February 18, 1936, local Cleveland Plain Dealer writer Alex Zirin wrote in his column that Johnny Risko was not yet finished as a fighter but had just about given up on any hope of meeting Joe Louis. However, Risko said he was willing to meet the Italian man mountain, Primo Carnera. According to Zirin;

"In a recent letter from Miami to his trainer, Freddy Rogers, Johnny expressed willingness to box Carnera."
—*Cleveland Plain Dealer* (2-18-36)

Johnny had planned to meet Carnera for one more payday and then exit the fight game. At least that was the word among his friends and family. But fighters always say they are quitting after one more bout and Johnny Risko apparently was no different.

In June of 1936, the boxing world saw one of the biggest upsets when former Heavyweight Champion Max Schmeling knocked out Joe Louis in twelve rounds. Louis had predicted a victory early by kayo but he couldn't seem to get out of the way of Max's lethal right hand bombs.

After Joe Louis suffered the humiliating defeat at the hands of Schmeling, Danny Dunn and Johnny Risko seemed all the more interested in meeting Joe Louis. However the Louis camp turned them down and Louis knocked out former champ Jack Sharkey in three rounds on August 18, 1936, at Yankee Stadium in New York. This was his first comeback fight and then in his second he took on Al Ettore and stopped him in five rounds on September 22nd in Philadelphia. It seemed Johnny Risko was totally out of the picture now.

Earlier in the month on September 11th, Johnny did make the papers but not because of any potential fights. Risko, who owned a tavern/restaurant on Lake Road in Sheffield Lake, Ohio was charged with selling beer after 1 a.m. on the previous July 5th. The Mayor of Sheffield Lake was taking his good old time preparing a written decision. When asked if there was any reason for the delay, he responded, "Yes," he said. "You see the lawyers asked for a written decision on the facts and findings and I'm preparing it, for I think they will appeal." Risko denied he had sold any beer in his place after the legal closing hour. "The mayor has it in for me," he said, "but I don't know why." —*Cleveland Plain Dealer* (9-11-36)

Just when it seemed the proposed Joe Louis-Johnny Risko bout was dead and buried talks began again. Suddenly the Louis camp felt that Risko would be a good fighter to add to their fighter's resume. According to the Cleveland Plain Dealer on September 24, 1936, the fight would be the main event of the annual Cleveland News Christmas Fund boxing show in Public Hall on December 14th.

Meanwhile on October 9th Louis had won a third comeback fight when he stopped the inexperienced Jorge Brescia in three rounds in New York. It was only Brescia's ninth pro fight.

Johnny often would be a spectator at fight shows when he wasn't actively fighting himself. On October 14, 1936, he attended a local fight show at the Central Armory. One particular bout involving local lightweights Jimmy Vaughn, whose real name was Paul James Cvecka, and Ray Sharkey, had a strange ending to the fight. A riot developed at ringside and soon chairs and other objects were flying through the air. Most everyone, except the two judges Herb Williams and Charles Bill, felt Sharkey won at least 7 of 10 rounds. Even the referee, former World Champion Johnny Kilbane, voted for Sharkey. When the decision was announced all hell broke loose. The chairs went sailing into the ring barely missing Johnny Kilbane. Seven squads of police were summoned and the officials and fighters were escorted to the dressing room. Johnny Risko observed the mayhem at ringside and remarked, "No wonder the game's on the bum here."

Promoters were expecting a record crowd in December for the Joe Louis-Johnny Risko fight. In spite of being inactive and having several proposed bouts canceled or not even officially scheduled, some felt that Risko would give the youngster from Detroit a very tough battle. Others felt with Risko's age and inactivity it was a mistake. Risko was said to have over $250,000 in his accounts, a fortune for the time and really didn't need to fight again. Even Danny Dunn felt Johnny should have a couple tune-up fights first. Risko felt confident and observers of his workouts said he was using his right hand a lot more. It became a mute point when on November 29th it was announced Risko had suffered a broken rib sparring and would not be able to meet Louis on December 14th. Sparring partner, young Ed Shelby, is the guy who did the deed. Johnny had complained of a sore rib two days previously but felt he could work through it. X-ray photographs however revealed that his eighth rib on his right side was fractured.

Local heavyweight Eddie Simms, who had been clamoring for a fight with Risko for a few years was selected as a replacement to meet Joe Louis on the December 14th Public Hall card. Simms had met many good fighters in his career and although not a push over, he certainly was not someone who would threaten the comeback of Joe Louis. But nobody expected what happened at the Christmas Fund show main event. Nearly 11,000 fans were on hand. The fight had barely started when after Simms threw a few feeble jabs at the stomach of Louis, and was squaring up to punch again, suddenly Louis landed a left hook on Simm's chin and down he went. When he arose, imported referee, Arthur Donovan asked him if he was okay. According to writer John Lardner's report in the December 15th *Cleveland Plain Dealer* , the conversation went as follows:

Donovan-- "How do you feel boy?"

Simms-- "Um"

Donovan-- "Can you see anything?"

Simms-- "I'll go. Will I go up on the roof now?"

Donovan-- "What did you say?"

Simms-- "Where do you want me to go?"

Donovan-- "All right, that's all."

The fight was stopped after just 26 seconds of the first round.

Johnny Risko may not have been battling in the ring but he was fighting a political battle in Sheffield Lake Village where he lived. Earlier Johnny had been cited for selling beer at his tavern after normal closing hours. Apparently he didn't like the mayor and the mayor didn't like him. He contested the salaries of local officials, including that of Mayor Harvey H. Dier, Clerk Frank Fields and Marshall William McKinley. But on January 30, 1937, Common Pleas Judge Guy R. Findley ruled in the officials favor.

Johnny's trainer, Freddy Rogers was fighting his own battle. He had opened a place called Ringside Cafe at St. Clair Avenue N.E. and East 32nd Street in Cleveland. In addition to the normal offerings of such an establishment he had begun to hold boxing exhibitions on Saturday nights. Apparently this had been going on for almost two years. This upset the Cleveland Boxing Commission who objected that Rogers had not even applied for a permit to stage boxing shows. In addition to that they said that they objected to (a) boxing in a cafe and (b) boxing on Saturday night. The chairman of the Cleveland Boxing Commission, the former great Major League baseball player and manager, Tris Speaker was asked why the commission had not objected before. His response was that the commission had just learned about it. Speaker said, "Of course, we don't approve a boxing show in connection with a saloon." Speaker went on to say, "That's a long-time ruling of the commission. I don't think it does the game any good. While I'm not in the liquor business myself, I don't think a saloon is a very good place to bring up young athletes." —*Cleveland Plain Dealer* (3-25-37)

On April 6, 1937, an AP story out of Miami Beach, Florida,

stated that Risko was ready to hit the comeback trail on account of the "bunch of bums that's fighting these days." Risko said that his plans were to fight out on the Pacific Coast. Risko was 34 years old at the time and weighed about 200 pounds but was said to be in fairly good condition, although he hadn't fought in two years. Risko went on to even further say that he wanted a crack at Jim Braddock. He was quoted as saying that Braddock would defeat Joe Louis when they eventually clashed. Johnny's big plans to fight in California came to an abrupt halt when on April 13, 1937, local scribe James E. Doyle wrote that Danny Dunn reported:

"The big guy got a busted ankle bone. Got it last Wednesday when his heel caught in some torn canvas in the mat of the ring he was working out on. That California trip is off."
—*Cleveland Plain Dealer* (4-13-37)

Risko's prediction that Jim Braddock would defeat Joe Louis on June 22nd, of course was not even close. Braddock put up a game effort, in fact floored Louis in the first minute of round one with a right uppercut. But by the end of the seventh round Braddock's face was swollen and battered and his manager Joe Gould wanted to stopped the fight. Jim Braddock had too much pride and wouldn't let him so he came out for the eighth round and eventually Louis landed a left to the body and a right hand to the jaw and Braddock landed face first and didn't move as he was counted out at 1:10 of the round. Louis was the new champion.

Johnny healed and time went by. He never seemed far from the newspapers, whether for a proposed match or involvement in functions. Johnny's Stop 84 in Sheffield Lake included Texaco gas pumps. He and his family were guests of the Texas Distributing Co. at a picnic at Geauga Lake Park. Geauga Lake was a local amusement park that often held big corporate picnics and events. A baseball tournament was included and various races. Winners included Johnny Risko and Betty Boehmer, Ohio Women's Ice Skating Champion. On August 30, 1937, Johnny attended an amateur boxing show at Brookside Stadium in Cleveland. Johnny Kilbane, Johnny Risko, and Carmen Barth were all asked to guest referee on the card. Events like this kept Johnny in the limelight.

Johnny and his wife, Margaret continued to battle local officials in Sheffield Lake over the official's salaries. Margaret Risko was interviewed about the local politics on October 17, 1937. (Plain Dealer Special) When asked if the Riskos were still in for the resolution, Mrs. Risko said: "Sure we are. We have a lot of property out here and taxes are high."

Johnny and Margaret Risko

Johnny's wife, like a lot of boxers wives, was often asked how she felt about her husband's comeback plans. On October 23rd she replied when asked if she was in favor of Johnny's. "In favor of it?" she said with a wry smile. "Why should I be? He was comfortably retired, and I must admit I was hoping he never would put on those gloves again. But Johnny doesn't like too much comfort I guess, at least he was getting terribly restless."

She went on to say "Then, after we went up to Detroit two weeks ago to see the tenth anniversary of boxing shows at the Olympia there, I could see that his mind was really made up. He got a great hand from the crowd--the biggest hand of all the fighters who were introduced, I'd say--and that settled it. It's not that I don't think he can still put up a pleasing fight--I'm sure he can--but, after all, what's the use? After all these years especially?"

"What, if by some strange chance." Mrs. Risko was asked. "Johnny should catch up with a fight with Joe Louis--the fight he wants so much?"
"Oh, that would be great." was the quick reply. "I've always thought myself that Joe Louis was made to order for him, as they say." —*Cleveland Plain Dealer* (10-23-37)

Whether Joe Louis was made to order or not, meeting Louis would have meant that Johnny Risko finally achieved his dream of fighting for the title. But this was not going to happen.

Finally in November Johnny Risko signed to meet former light-heavyweight champion, Bob Olin, at Central Armory in Cleveland. On November 9th Gordon Cobbledick wrote in his Cleveland Plain Dealer column that Danny Dunn said the only reason Johnny was fighting was because he was "jealous" of Joe Louis. Dunn reported when asked what he thought about the possibility his comeback fight against Bob Olin would turn out less than satisfactory that Risko replied: "Get another fight" he grunted. "What the hell." —*Cleveland Plain Dealer* (11-9-37)

Leading up to the Olin fight it was reported that in training Johnny was using his right hand a lot more than usual. In 1924 when he ruined his right shoulder in the Homer Smith fight, it changed Risko's style of fighting. His right hand ended up a secondary weapon as opposed to the main one he had during his amateur days.

And interesting story appeared in James E. Doyle's *Cleveland Plain Dealer* column on November 17, 1937. It was titled as follows:

Don't Worry About John

"Not a few of the citizens have been shaking their heads sadly and declaring that Johnny Risko must be punch-drunk-else why would all the money he'll be needing in this world, did he obey that impulse to return to the ring after a virtual three-year layoff?

But the truth is that the old boy is a smarter Johnny Risko today than ever he was in the days when he was mauling his merry way to the fortune that won't get away from him. Also it is true that he's something of a hard-headed freak. Were he

not, he'd have been battered balmy long since.
No, Johnny isn't walking on his heels. Ding-toed, as always, he's on those ding-toes most of the time.

"I guess it's true," he admits modestly, "what somebody said years ago. Instead of havin' the brains punched out of me, like so many poor guys in the ring, I guess it's a fact I had a few punched into me."

Risko scored what perhaps was his last significant victory on November 17th when he bullied his way to a ten-round decision over the former champion Olin in Cleveland. Although Risko showed the effects of his long absence from the ring, he was aggressive and showed his old-time ability in the infighting. He was unmarked at the end of the bout. Risko weighed 195 pounds and Olin 185 1/2. It was a good victory for Risko, made him confident and feel relevant once again.

Risko ducks under an attack from Bob Olin.
(Cleveland Public Library photo)

(above) The victor (over Olin) with his manager, Danny Dunn (Author's collection)

On December 2, 1937, Johnny Risko's father once again appeared in the local newspapers. Apparently John Risko Sr. was fined in Lorain County Court $50.00 for socking a village marshal who attempted to arrest him. The Deputy Marshal H.J. Miller found the elder Risko in an argumentative mood when he attempted to take him to jail for creating a disturbance.

Danny Dunn lined up a second comeback fight for Johnny on December 10, 1937, in Lima, Ohio. His opponent was listed as one Jimmy Delaney of Buffalo, New York. It wasn't much of a fight as Risko pounded Delaney to the deck three times in the third round. In the fourth round he finished off Delaney in one minute to end the fight. Doing research for this book I have no idea who this opponent Jimmy Delaney actually was. The real Jimmy Delaney, the famous one anyway, was from Minnesota and had actually won a newspaper decision over Johnny Risko in 1926, in Minneapolis. He retired in 1927. I could not find a boxing record for this "Jimmy Delaney from Buffalo, New York".

The Risko camp all along said they had their sights set on meeting the World Light-heavyweight Champion, John Henry Lewis. The match was set for December 17, 1937, in Cleveland at Public Hall. Lewis, in this writers opinion, was and is one of the most underrated champions of his division. He had 117 fights and only lost 8 of them, while winning 60 by knockout. After winning the World Light-heavy title from Bob Olin in 1935, he defended it five times before giving it up to fight Joe Louis for the heavyweight title in 1939. Lewis was knocked out in one round (the only time he was ever stopped) and he retired. But when he fought Johnny Risko in 1937 he was still the champion and on top of his game.

On December 17, 1937, Johnny Risko took on John Henry Lewis in what he hoped would be a fight to launch him back into the list of contenders. Somebody apparently forgot to tell John Henry Lewis that because Lewis out-smarted, out-fought and out-gamed the Rubber Man. The 23-year old Light-heavy Champion had too much skill and youth on his side for the 35-year old Risko. Johnny as always tried hard but it was apparent he just didn't have it. According to a ringside count by Everett M. Tyler of the Cleveland Call and Post, Risko only landed four flush blows in the entire ten rounds.

In early January of 1938, Mike Jacobs highest man in the promotions business was in Cleveland to watch bike races at the new Cleveland Arena at East 37th and Euclid Avenue. When the subject of Johnny Risko came up Jacob's answered quickly and to the point: "Johnny Risko made an awful, awful mistake in grabbin' that match with Light Heavy Champ John Henry Lewis. That fixed Johnny as far as a bout with Joe Louis is concerned-and I have been givin' a lot of thought to putting that one on in Detroit."

After the Lewis bout Johnny Risko took on a series of fights mostly in the south. He had been spending his winters in Miami, Florida, where he enjoyed playing rummy at the Elks Club. After the Lewis defeat he headed off once again to the sunshine for a good rest. He was still not admitting he was finished fighting and there wasn't any talk on his part of retiring. His wife was vacationing with him in February of

1938, and was asked about her never-say-quit spouse by reporters. She was also pleased to hear from the reporters that Mr. and Mrs. James Braddock were expected to arrive there shortly. There was a recipe you see that Mrs. Risko wanted to borrow from Mrs. Braddock. "How, Mrs. Braddock, did you manage to convince your husband that it was time for him to leave the ring? And he is only 32!" But Johnny apparently wasn't ready to quit.

The years 1938 to early 1940 surely did not provide Johnny Risko with a grand exit from the fight game. Quite the contrary he had ten fights and finished with a 6-4 record in those bouts. What's more important is, except for two of those contests, his opponents were mostly has-beens and several who could be considered "Never was". On February 3, 1938, Risko met a fighter named George Brown in Miami Beach and won by a 3rd round knockout. Brown's career record ended up 14-26. On February 22, 1938, Johnny met a pretty good fighter in one Clarence "Red" Burman. They were matched in Coral Gables, Florida. During his career Burman won 78 fights and lost 22, with 2 draws. He also would have the honor of meeting Joe Louis for the heavyweight title in 1941. Although stopped in the fifth round, at least he got a shot. Burman had an easy time with Risko, decisively outpointing him. Burman, who weighed 181 pounds to Risko's 193, won every round on the scorecards.

    The newspaper reports said Risko was slow and failed to land a single hard blow. After the fight Risko's face was a bunch of bumps, cuts and bruises. He greeted his wife and she was happy to report to the newspapermen that this was indeed Johnny's last fight. If it had only been so, little did she know that the Cleveland Rubber Man was not through bouncing around quite yet.

There was a little note in James E. Doyle's column in The *Cleveland Plain Dealer,* on June 28, 1938. Johnny Risko had purchased a restaurant and bar in Miami. Doyle quipped "Risk' His Own Bouncer?"

Tragedy struck the Risko family on July 7, 1938, when a niece of Johnny's, Arlene Cifranic drowned in a fish pond in the front yard of the Risko home in Sheffield Lake. She was only two-and-a-half. Her mother Mrs. Peter Cifranic had brought her up from the beach at the rear of the Risko home and had put her in the yard. Fifteen minutes later she looked for her and found her in the pond. There was a small fence around the pond but apparently the child climbed over it. Her father, a member of the Sheffield Village Fire Department, tried artificial respiration but it failed to revive his daughter.

The Cleveland Rubber Man had obviously lost his ability to defeat a fighter of any importance. One note in the Cleveland Plain Dealer by a reader to the sports editor was titled Rubber Czech? "Johnny Risko is really Czechoslovakian," says Woodland Hill Billy, "so how is it that nobody ever thought o' callin' him the Cleveland Rubber Czech?"

Risko could not land any fights the rest of 1938. He kept busy with his new place in Miami, which was said to feature the biggest sandwiches anywhere. He played cards at the Elks Club and golfed. Occasionally he was asked to referee fights as he did on October 27th in Miami for a bout between Johnny Dean of Philadelphia and Indian Johnny

Heavyweight contender, Tony Musto

Johnny Risko cools off after another hard training session.

Lindsey of Ponca City, Oklahoma. The hardest work he had to do in that fight was carry Lindsey to his corner after Dean stopped him in the second round.

In November of 1938, it was announced that Risko had added a "Book-stall" in his eating and drinking establishment in Miami. We are not talking about library books here. Risko said: "They're betting pretty good into my book already", in a local newspaper story on November 19th.

1939 started off slowly with no fights for Risko until he met Bob Sikes on July 26th in Pine Bluff, Arkansas. Sikes won the 10-round decision. It was Sikes 10th professional bout. Johnny weighed 200 pounds, eleven more than Sikes. On August 3rd Johnny's opponent was a guy named Young Allen in Macon, Georgia. Once again Risko lost the decision. And once again Johnny lost to a fighter who was only engaging in his 9th pro fight. Allen ended up 8-12-2 in his less than stellar career.

August 15, 1939, found the road show continuing as Battling Blackjack fell in three rounds in Tucson, Arizona. And yes, the Battling one was only fighting for the 9th time and was outweighed by nineteen pounds. The sideshow continued in Phoenix on August 18th as Babe Daniels was stopped in four rounds. Babe managed a record of 1-4-2 in his career. Johnny had hoped to fight out in California and even though he was attempting to keep busy, California officials were less than impressed.

On September 3, 1939, the Associated Press printed the following in the *Cleveland Plain Dealer*:

"Risko Is Denied Boxing License

San Francisco, Sept. 2- (AP)--Johnny Risko, the veteran Cleveland heavyweight boxer, has been denied a license to box in California.

Don Shields, chief inspector of the State Athletic Commission, said today Risko's age (36) and the fact he has been out of the game too long were the reasons for the refusal."

Risko's next opponent at least had more than a handful of fights. His Fort Smith, Arkansas opponent was one Sandy McDonald who offered no real opposition and Johnny won in ten rounds. They met on October 2nd. McDonald finished his career at 24-34-4 and was stopped 24 times. The end was near yet Risko continued to fight on. On December 14, 1939, Johnny finished out the year in Aiken, South Carolina against Jack Lawton. Risko won by a 4th round knockout against a man who had exactly two fights in his professional career and was stopped both times.

Why oh why did Risko continue to fight? I wish I knew. If 1938 and 1939 were not embarrassing enough Johnny had two fights in 1940. At 38 years of age he really should not have been fighting. But on January 29, 1940, he once again met Sandy McDonald, this time in Hot Springs, Arkansas. Risko's ten round decision win over McDonald would prove to be his last career victory.

On February 19, 1940, Johnny Risko went to the well one time too many. His opponent in Miami Beach, Florida was Tony Musto. Early in his career Musto was a pretty good fighter. During his career he managed to defeat such fighters as Curtis Sheppard, Lee Savold, Lem Franklin and Jimmy Bivins. He even met Joe Louis for the heavyweight title in 1941, and put up a brave battle while it lasted. That fight was halted in the 6th round to save the "Blue Island Tank" from further punishment. When Musto met Risko, he was only 23 years old and the Cleveland Rubber Man was 38. Risko's weight was good at 197 1/2 pounds. Musto weighed in at 201.

Although most everyone who followed boxing realized that Johnny Risko was at the end of his career, I don't think anyone would have expected the way the fight would end. Musto basically had his way with Risko, actually picked him up one time and slammed him into the corner. Musto staggered Johnny several times, hit him with two huge right hands in round two. But when he landed a right uppercut in the third round that dropped Johnny nobody expected that referee Eddie Coachman would toll the ten count over him. The Rubber Man couldn't get up and thus the fight ended. It was the only knockout blemish in Risko's long career. Risko was stopped in nine rounds via a technical knockout against Max Schmeling in 1929 and was involved with a controversial fight with Chuck Wiggins in 1925 that sometimes is listed as a knockout or technical knockout and sometimes not. The Musto knockout is the only official knockout for the count that Johnny Risko ever suffered. Musto ended up his career with only thirteen knockouts, so his stoppage of Risko must have really registered with Johnny. It was a sad ending to a long and sometimes stellar career. Johnny finally realized it was the end.

Johnny Risko makes the news.

Retirement

The Tony Musto loss convinced Johnny Risko that it was time to hang up the gloves once and for all. His last few years in the ring were futile at best and in this writer's opinion mostly an embarrassment.
Although Johnny officially retired after the Musto match he did not fade from public view. Often he was asked to referee a match, many times it was wrestling or rasslin' as I like to call it. And his name did not disappear from the newspapers. In early 1940 a small article appeared in the Cleveland Plain Dealer by Alva Johnson of the Saturday Evening Post regarding the great actor and movie director Orson Wells. Johnson went on to say, "Wells can pour himself into a mold like gelatin. His face has an ectoplasmic elasticity like Laughton's; his physique resembles that of Fighting Baker of Cleveland, known as "rubbery, blubbery John Risko."

Just as his name would appear in the papers regarding a speeding ticket or other legal matters concerning his establishments, he also appeared in the Cleveland Plain Dealer regarding a lawsuit he filed against his longtime manager, Danny Dunn. Dunn's sister, Mrs. Sarah A. Sheridan, asked the Plain Dealer to explain that $2,400 for which Dunn was being sued was not a debt of Dunn's but of hers. She explained in a letter that Risko lent her the money so she could meet a mortgage on the Vernona (N.J.) farm where she and her husband lived and where Risko trained for many of his fights. Dunn had been merely co-signer of the note. (Cleveland Plain Dealer 11-15-40)

On December 2, 1940, Tony Musto, conqueror of Johnny Risko in what would be the final fight of the Cleveland Rubber Man, was matched with Chilean, Arturo Godoy at the Cleveland Arena. Godoy, looking for a third match with Joe Louis, gave Musto a real pasting, flooring him twice in the fifth round and battering him throughout. On December 6, 1940, in a *Cleveland Plain Dealer* column, Risko's trainer for the last twelve years of his career, Freddy Rogers, was asked how Johnny would have fared in his fighting prime against Godoy. It appeared as follows:

"If Godoy Had Met Risk' Little Mr. Freddy Rogers, who served as training director and head rubber for old Rubber Man Johnny Risko in the days when the Risk' was in his ring prime, gave a keenly interested eye to the wild walloping bee of Arturo Godoy and Tony Musto at the Arena last Monday, because the Must' had been ballyhooed as a second Risk.

'That fat little guy out o' Chicago has got a heart like ol' Johnny's, at that,' said Mr. Rogers afterward, 'and he's built somethin' like him, for a fact, but that about let's him out, as far as comparin' is concerned.

I'd like to seen Mr. Godoy tryin' to belt the ribs and kidneys out o' Johnny, the way he did out o' Musto. He'd found out what a real rough-house was like. And he'd prob'ly wound up like big George Godfrey did after he'd slammed Johnny's slats for five or six rounds. I mean he'd prob'ly wound up lookin' for the quickest way out o' that ring.

Yessir, Johnny would o' put a chill on that Chilean's heart. How he did like to meet up with them big guys that thought they were the bulliest boys in all the world! He'd just laugh in their mugs, tell 'em to cut loose with ev'rything they had-and then when they got weary, he'd come on like Man o' War and bust their hearts completely.'"

On July 12, 1941, a small article appeared in the Cleveland Plain Dealer announcing that Johnny's wife, Margaret had filed for a divorce. The article appeared as follows:

"Johnny Risko, Cleveland's famous Rubber Man of boxing, said he knew "nothing about it" when informed last night that his wife, Margaret E. Risko, had filed suit for divorce in Miami, Fla., last Saturday.

Risko said he had last seen his wife in Miami a month ago and hadn't heard from her since.

Mrs. Risko, who married the heavyweight title contender in

Cleveland, May 5, 1930, charged that Risko "became sullen and morose and indulged in harsh words," according to the Associated Press. She listed her address as Stop 84, Lake Road, Lorain, O., where Risko now is staying."

A short time later, on November 8, 1941, Johnny Risko posted a notice in *The Cleveland Plain Dealer*:

"ON and after this date I will not be responsible for debts contracted by anyone other than myself. JOHN RISKO, 2008 Eglindale."

On August 12, 1942, Johnny answered his country's call and joined the United States Army. He had been recruited by former heavyweight champ, Gene Tunney to join the Navy, but Johnny elected to join the Army. When asked why he hadn't accepted an invitation from Gene Tunney to join the Navy, he replied:

"Because I don't like boats; that's all. Never did. Wouldn't give a dollar for the best boat in the world. Ask some people who tried to sell me some good ones for the lake. Maybe I will have to go on one or two boats with the Army, but that will be different. No kick." —Cleveland Plain Dealer (8-24-42)

On August 27, 1942, Johnny left for the Army. Although he was 40 years old he felt he needed to carry on the fight for the country he had made his home since he was very young. Earlier Johnny wrote his former trainer, Freddy Rogers and told him, "I understand that I probably could get out of the Army soon if I wanted to. But none of that out for me, kid. Here's one scrap that's GOT to be won, and this anti-aircraft gunner is going through." Although weighing 245 lbs. he went through the rigors of Army Boot Camp. An article appeared in the Cleveland Plain Dealer on December 3, 1942, stating Johnny Risko had won another medal.....a sharpshooter's medal for his rifle training.

Johnny was asked several times to talk on the radio and he obliged. He was on the radio at Camp Perry, Ohio, later in a Norfolk broadcast, another time at Newport News, both times when he was stationed at Fort Eustis, Virginia. Johnny's weight slowly came down and he was quoted in February of 1943, as saying, "I am almost in fighting condition once more. We did 25 miles on the road and over hill and dale with full field pack the other day. Two days later we ran seven and a half miles in an hour and a half. It looks like bad news for the Axis." (*Cleveland Plain Dealer* 2-25-43)

On March 27, 1943, a story appeared in the *Cleveland Plain Dealer*:

"JOHNNY RISKO GIVEN OVER-AGE DISCHARGE

CAMP DAVIS, N.C., March 26-

(UP)–Pvt. Johnny Risko, 40-year-old former heavyweight boxer who retired from the ring in 1937 after some 350 bouts as the "Cleveland Rubber Man," left here today under the Army's over-age discharge law to take a job in a Lorain (O.) defense plant.

Camp public relations officers said the veteran fighter was

one of many enlisted men 38 or more years old being released from military service at this antiaircraft artillery training center. He has been in uniform for nearly a year."

James E. Doyle's column in the *Cleveland Plain Dealer* on March 31, 1943, covering Risko's discharge from the Army appeared as follows:

Johnny Risko Cried

"I cried for the first time in my life," says Johnny Risko.

"And I ain't ashamed to admit it. Big tears I cried–when I said goodby to all them kids I'd soldiered with for seven months.

Some of the kids cried too. They was good friends of mine. And one of them said: 'The hell with your 40 years, John! You're still tough enough for any army in the world.'

But the captain said, 'No, John. That ol' left leg of yours can't take 245 lbs. It's tough John,' he said, 'but you're going home.'

The captain was a good guy too."

On April 1, 1943, it was announced that Johnny Risko would become an employee of the Lorain Brass Co., in Elyria, Ohio. That same night he attended the Lloyd Marshall-Ezzard Charles match at the Cleveland Arena. He received a great hand when he was introduced from the ring before the main event.

By July of 1943, Johnny had gotten his weight down

to 200 lbs. He had been working out regularly with his old trainer, Freddy Rogers in an open-air ring out in Parma, Ohio. Someone asked Risko if he was thinking of coming back and Johnny was quoted in the *Cleveland Plain Dealer* on July 2, 1943, as saying, "Could be thinkin' like that," was the reply, "but just for one fight. There's a fat old slob I'm sure I could still trim. His name is Galento."

Risko's reckless driving got the better of him once again when he was pulled over in early December of 1943. He was charged with hitting 50 miles an hour and his gasoline rations were suspended for 15 days on his resultant appearance before Chairman Don Whyte of the Lorain War Price and Rationing Board.

Johnny Risko's driving exploits always were a part of his public life. On January 1, 1944, his name appeared once again in the *Cleveland Plain Dealer.* Apparently he fell asleep at the wheel of his car the day before and crashed into a post in Avon Lake, Ohio. He suffered a laceration of his chin and a broken left arm. He was kept over night in Lorain St. Joseph's Hospital, where he was held for further observation. His condition was listed as "good".

In the summer of 1944, Johnny added to his list of businesses when he invested in a portion of a night club in Lakewood, Ohio. He called it the Coconut Grove. Johnny always seemed restless and kept busy with his ventures. He also loved to place a few bets on the horse races, both in Cleveland and elsewhere. He won a nice piece of change on a horse named Bold Risk, in the summer of 1944. One of the local horse players said that horse could have been named for the ring game's dauntless Cleveland Rubber Man.

In late October of 1944, a memorial service was held at Martin Luther Church, 2135 W. 14th Street, in Cleveland, for Johnny's brother Sergeant Paul Risko, who had been killed in France during World War II. I remember talking to one of the 'oldtimers' years ago. I remember him saying how much it saddened the Rubber Man that his kid brother was gone and he couldn't serve his country to avenge his death. Paul was said to be quite the musician, also organized and led orchestras. As mentioned previously he tried his hand at amateur boxing but never went far. Eventually Paul ended up in the United States Army. Shortly after the troops landed at Normandy on D Day, Sgt. Paul Risko was killed in Northern France on July 29, 1944. Paul Risko is believed to be the first casualty from the 86th and 6th Calvary Reconnaissance Squadron during World War II. He is buried in the American Cemetery at Normandy.

The author pays his respects at the grave of Paul Risko (Normandy, 2015 - Lynda Bibler photo)

Johnny Risko: The Cleveland Rubber Man

A strange ad appeared in the *Cleveland Plain Dealer* Lost and Found section on November 19, 1944:

"LOST: Feather quilt. 2 pillows, sheet, bed-pad wrapped in sheet. Wednesday night between Rocky River and Sheffield Village. Reward. Risko Stop 84, Lake Rd."

I don't know what occurred or how, but the Risko name never seemed to be far from public view.

On March 2, 1945, a story appeared in the Cleveland Plain Dealer stating Steve Dudas and Tony Musto were both planning returns to the ring wars. When Johnny was asked if he planned a return he said, "I ain't the solid Rubber Man I used to be, but I s'pose I still could do as good in that ring, if I didn't know enough to keep out, as them other gray-whiskered guys."

Johnny's mother died on July 7, 1945. She had been helping run Stop 84, the tavern and restaurant on Lake Rd. in Sheffield Lake, Ohio. The property also included Texaco Gas pumps out front. Johnny's sister, Mary Risko had a beauty shop next door. My neighbor, Dorothy Lloyd was once married to Richard Cifranic, nephew of Johnny Risko. In 1952 she recalled that the property on Lake Rd. had two houses, one large, one smaller. She also stated at one time she thought Johnny had a training camp on the property.

She only met Johnny Risko a few times but she recalled that while she and her husband were having their house built in 1952, Johnny showed up with his boxer dog, and was in their house when something got the dogs attention and he (Johnny) ran into the bathroom and out the window. Thankfully there was no glass in the window yet. Dorothy recalled that at one time she kept the books for the family businesses.

According to Dorothy her mother-in-law and Johnny, along with his father, ran the business and when Johnny passed in 1953, the place became Susan Cifranic's, her mother-in-law's. Although not owned by any members of the Risko family today, Risko's Tavern remains on the property with the same name it has had for well over seventy-five years. I have visited there and sadly there is no indication that Johnny Risko ever owned the place, no photos, no memorabilia.

Johnny Risko's Bar.
'Risko's' in name only - it could do with some momentos or photographs honoring its previous owner (Author's photo).

Sometime in 1946, Johnny married for a second time. His wife, the former Mildred Weber met Johnny when she ran the Dew Drop Lunch at 1760 W. 25th Street, Cleveland. Johnny was a regular customer there. It was the second marriage for both of them.

Danny Dunn suffered a heart attack in early 1946. He recovered and was never lost for words when talking about his "big fella". He had been flat on his back for almost four months but managed to make his way down to the Cleveland Plain Dealer to talk over old times with James E. Doyle. It can't be minimized to state that Danny Dunn, an ex-pug, who came across as gruff and rough at times, was indeed a rare gem in the world of boxing managers. Not only did he guide Johnny Risko to some great victories, he also took care of him financially. Rare is it to hear feel-good stories about former fighters who were not broke or down on their luck.
Johnny branched out in many areas during his retirement. He remained popular and was always asked his opinion of fighters, race horses or other newsworthy things. He was asked to be a guest speaker and even landed a coaching job at the Karamu Studio Theatre in Cleveland, in early 1947, as boxing coach for the lead actor, George Livingstone, who was appearing in 'Golden Boy'.

Johnny Risko was said to be well heeled when he retired from the ring. He was not afraid to spend his money and often bet on the horses. As the May 3, 1947, Kentucky Derby approached, Johnny bragged to all his friends he had a sure thing on a horse named "Riskolator". Unfortunately the horse finished eleventh out of thirteen entries.
In early August of 1947, former opponent George Godfrey passed away. He was said to be down-and-out when he died. James E. Doyle, famed writer of the *Cleveland Plain Dealer*,

recalled in his August 15, 1947, column how he attended the Godfrey-Risko match at Ebbets Field in Brooklyn, New York, in 1928. There he met former heavyweight champion, Jim Corbett and famous announcer Joe Humphries. Both of them felt Risko didn't have a chance against the giant Godfrey. The bettors felt the same way. Obviously somebody cleaned up when Johnny won the match. Doyle recalled how Risko, a big baseball fan said, "I've always wanted to see this Brooklyn ball park," grinned Johnny, "and I s'pose this is as good a way as any other to be seein' it. Yup, this'll be all right. There'll be some heavy hittin' at Ebbetts (sic) Field tonight."
—*Cleveland Plain Dealer (8-15-47)*

Johnny loved to be remembered and was often quoted in the papers. On November 11, 1947, he attended the Pat Comiskey-Big Boy Brown fight at the Cleveland Arena. The next day in the Cleveland Plain Dealer a small story appeared. Brown, who weighed over 260 lbs., was stopped via a knockout in the fifth round. Risko was sitting at ringside and almost fell out of his chair laughing at the defensive maneuvers of the corpulent catcher from Tigertown. "They used to call me the Cleveland Rubber Man," said the old-timer, a fellow by the name of Risko. "Now you're lookin' at the Detroit Blubber Man." —*Cleveland Plain Dealer (11-14-47)*

Risko was not content in spending his money in one place. In early 1948, he went down to New Orleans to bet the horse races. Thinking he was getting away from the cold Cleveland winter, he suddenly found himself in 10 degrees above zero weather in the Crescent City. Johnny quipped that he might have to move over to Florida to stop shivering.

Johnny obviously didn't follow the career records of current fighters after he retired. When asked in February of 1949, while attending the Blackjack Billy Fox-Dick Wagner fight at the Cleveland Arena, what he felt about the future of Fox, Risko replied something to the effect that he felt the Fox management team was bringing their fighter along too quickly. Fact of the matter heading into the Cleveland fight Fox had been fighting since 1943, with well over 50 bouts.

Johnny was always a guy who the sports writers would ask opinions of when a big fight was coming up. When asked in September of 1950 who he felt would win the Ezzard Charles-Joe Louis contest, he didn't hesitate to say it would be Louis. He felt that even at his advanced age of 36, Louis had too much fire power for Charles. Of course he was wrong.

Johnny and his second wife, Mildred, attend the News 'Toyshop Fund' show.

(December, 1950)

An article in the *Cleveland Plain Dealer* on January 20, 1951, was titled 'Gone Are the Days'. The whole point of the story was to say that Johnny Risko was born 20 to 25 years too soon, that if he was fighting during the current time he would have cleaned up. Risko's response was straight to the point:

"Wha'd'ya mean I was born that much too soon? What money is there in what's left of the fight game now? No sir; you're all wrong. Ev'rybody could make a nice buck in my time. Ev'rybody who was any good a'tall, I mean. And what kick would I get out of fightin' now, compared with the kick that went with battlin' guys like Tunney, Sharkey, Walker, Godfrey, Paulino and all of the rest of that kind? No, I got no complaints about when I was born. I couldn't of picked a better time if I'd had any say about it myself." —*Cleveland Plain Dealer (1-20-51)*

On May 4, 1951, Johnny went to a Cleveland Indians game. The 48-year old Risko got very ill at the game. He tried to laugh it off but apparently he had a heart attack. On May 11th he was still in the hospital in an oxygen tent and only his wife and two close friends were allowed to visit him. While in the hospital, fellow Clevelander, World Light-heavyweight Champ, Joey Maxim, who was in Chicago training for his heavyweight title fight with Ezzard Charles, sent a telegram to Risko. His message read:

"Sorry to learn you won't be able to be here when I win the title that you should have won for Cleveland long ago. I'm as confident this time as the Cleveland Rubber Man always used to be."

Said the Risk' to his nurse: "He'll do it too. If he comes out of his shell and doesn't forget he's got a right hand as well as a left." —*Cleveland PlainDealer (5-22-51)*

By early June Johnny was back to work. The *Cleveland Plain Dealer* reported on June 12, 1951:

"RUBBER MAN BOUNCES BACK."

"He was at his place on West 25th Street, greeting thirsty customers and looking hale and happy. He said however: "I almost had a terrible relapse," said Johnny, "on one of my last nights at the hospital. That was from watchin' the Charles-Maxim fight on a television that some well-meaning friends had brought into my room."

During Johnny Risko's retirement years he usually spent winters in Miami Beach, Florida. He was an avid member of the Elks Club and loved to play cards and bet on the horses. He had his Cleveland businesses and family but he loved the warm weather of Florida. He had made a lot of friends down there and they kept him busy. He had sold his interest in his Lakewood (Ohio) tavern, Coconut Grove, in 1951. He always seemed to be involved in one business or another. At one time or another he had a place on West 25th and another one at a different location on Detroit Avenue, plus Stop 84 in Sheffield Lake.

After selling his tavern in the summer of 1952, Johnny must have become bored because he went back to the horses, something per his doctor's advice, he had given up while recuperating from his heart issues. Risko claimed he didn't sell his tavern so he could have more time for leisurely pursuits like betting on the ponies. He claimed he had an offer so fat he couldn't turn it down.

Johnny Risko didn't always pick the winners when it came to horses, nor did he pick winners of the current fight scene. He picked Joe Louis to defeat Ezzard Charles, he picked Joey Maxim to beat the same Ezzard Charles, just to name a few. But when the up and coming Rocky Marciano was meeting Joe Louis he had him to win, and predicted Marciano would do the same thing to champion, Jersey Joe Walcott when they met for the title on September 23, 1952.

Johnny was quoted in the *Cleveland Plain Dealer* on September 9, 1952:

"What I like about young Marciano," says Johnny, "is that he fights just the way I used to fight. Rippin' and tearin' from one bell to the other, givin' the people a run for their money all the way, and just between the few of us, I wouldn't be surprised if he's even more of holy tearer than I was."

Johnny Risko saw a lot of himself in Rocky Marciano, probably for many reasons. Marciano was molded by little Charley Goldman, the same trainer who worked with Johnny in all of his fights in New York.

On January 13, 1953, Johnny and his wife Mildred were vacationing in Miami, Florida. They went to a meeting at the Elks Lodge and Johnny was sitting with his wife, Mildred, and friends, when he suffered a heart attack. Johnny was given oxygen on his way to the hospital but this time he didn't make it.

Risko's body was flown up to Cleveland and his funeral was set for January 17, 1953. The services were conducted by members of the Lakewood (Ohio) Elks Club, the lodge which Risko joined in 1931 at the height of his ring career. The Berry Funeral Home at 7200 Detroit Avenue handled the arrangements. A long line of cars, accompanying the body to its final resting place in Brooklyn Heights Cemetery in Cleveland, tied up traffic for several blocks in the Detroit-W. 65th area of Cleveland. Risko was survived by his wife, Mildred; his father, John C.; and two sisters, Mrs. Mary Forma and Mrs. Susan Cifranic.

Every sports figure and politician of note attended the funeral. Risko was remembered by many of his followers and fellow boxing fraternity, including then Cleveland Boxing Commissioner, Andrew G, Putka, Ollie Downs, commission secretary and President Max Neidenbach, of the Amateur Boxing Trainers Association, along with Secretary Phil Goldstein.

Cleveland Plain Dealer sports writer James E. Doyle, who had penned so many stories on the Cleveland Rubber Man, wrote in his column that he had received a postcard mailed on January 8 from Miami Beach, from Johnny. It simply said,

"They have been running the wrong way for me so far but I am hoping to get a good one." —*Johnny Risko*.
Doyle went on to say, "He was a good old friend, one of the best, and that last word from him is one that I'll be saving.

Hoping he got a good one, and the last big hearty laugh that would have gone with it. If you knew Johnny well, you still can hear that rumbling roaring laugh of his, and you remember that he liked to laugh every bit as much as he liked to fight. And what a fighter he was, between laughs!"

Gordon Cobbledick, Sports Editor of the Plain Dealer, wrote in his column on January 15, 1953, "There was a time, back in the late 20s, when almost any list of contenders for the heavyweight championship could have carried an asterisk before each name and a footnote reading: "Has been beaten by Risko." "That list would have included: Jack Sharkey, George Godfrey, Jimmy Maloney, Paulino Uzcudun, Jack Delaney, Tom Heeney, Max Baer and Tony Galento."

On March 21, 1953, Johnny Risko's will was read. He left all of his holdings to his wife, Mildred. A preliminary estimate said his estate was $10,000. However it was reported his other holdings were in his wife's name.

As mentioned Johnny Risko was one of four children of John Risko Sr. and Susie Risko (nee Macko) with sisters Susan and Mary and his younger brother Paul. Johnny Risko left a legacy in Cleveland and national boxing. He fought them all and he did it the right way. He and his manager, Danny Dunn would not play ball with the Tex Rickard or Mike Jacobs or anyone's monopoly. It may have cost them a shot at the title but it didn't cost them the respect of all who knew them.

CHEERS!
Johnny Risko serves up a cold one at one of the many bars he owned and operated.

Johnny Risko poses with the coveted championship belt.

Appendix

"Cleveland Rubber Man"

Born: August 18, 1902 Austria-Hungary

Died: January 13, 1953, Miami Beach, FL

Manager: Danny Dunn

Height 5-11 (5-10 1/2?)
Weight: 184-210

Pro Record: 67-42-5 (21 kayos) 25 ND, 1 NC

*Early Record Incomplete

1924

Mar 18	Wild Bill Reed	Lorain, OH	ND 10
Apr 7	Harry Krohn	Lorain, OH	TKO 9
Apr 23	Sam Dennis	Cleveland	KO 2
Apr 29	Mike Wallace	Lorain, OH	KO 2
May 25	Warren "Bumbo" Myers	Massilion, OH	KO 1
Jun 2	Homer Smith	Lorain, OH	ND 10
Sep 9	Joe Downey	Canton, OH	KO 5
Oct 1	Martin Burke	Cleveland	ND 10
Oct 7	Joe Lohman	Mansfield, OH	ND 10
Oct 10	Billy Walsh	Cleveland	KO 1
Oct 24	Battling Jack Dempsey	Barberton, OH	KO 6
Nov 28	Quintin Romero Rojas	Cleveland	ND 12

1925

Jan 26	Joe Lohman	Toledo, OH	ND 12

Bout may have taken place January 16

Feb 11	Sully Montgomery	Cleveland	ND 12
Feb 16	"Wild" Burt Kenny	Canton, OH	TKO 7
Mar 2	Joe Lohman	Cincinnati	ND 10
Apr 16	Jack Nolan	Meadville, PA	KO 6
May 30	Jack Renault	Cleveland	ND 12
Jun 16	Andy "Butch" Carr	Harrison, IN	TKO 8
Jun 24	Jack Clifford	Toledo, OH	ND 12
Jul 12	Young Stribling	Chicago	ND 10
Jul 17	Pedro Lopez	Wheeling, WV	KO 9
Jul 23	Jack McDonald	Harrison, IN	KO 3
Sep 9	Chuck Wiggins	Indianapolis	*LK 5

*This bout took place at Ft. Benjamin Harrison, which had no Boxing Commission; Risko was hit low and carried from the ring; the doctor gave him 25 minutes to recover and return to the bout, Risko's manager refused to let him continue.

Sep 17	Jack Sharkey	Boston	L 10
Nov 4	Chuck Wiggins	Indianapolis	ND 12
Nov 18	Gene Tunney	Cleveland	ND 12

Dec 11	Battling Gahee	Erie, PA	W 10

1926

Jan 4	Young Bob Fitzsimmons	Cleveland	ND 12
Feb 5	Jack Delaney	New York	L 10
Mar 19	Paul Berlenbach	New York	W 10
Apr 19	Quintin Romero Rojas	Buffalo	W 10
May 14	Young Stribling	New York	L 10
Jun 16	Leo Gates	Cleveland	LF 5
Jul 1	Mike McTigue	New York	L 10
Jul 13	King Solomon	St. Louis	ND 10
Jul 30	Tommy Loughran	Boston	L 10
Aug 10	Leo Gates	Harrison, IN	ND 10
Aug 26	Harry Persson	New York	L 10
Sep 10	Pat McCarthy	Hartford	D 10
Sep 20	Bob Lawson	Fremont, OH	ND 12
Sep 30	George Manley	Denver	D 4
Oct 12	Eddie Huffman	San Francisco	W 10
Oct 26	George Manley	Denver	L 4
Nov 12	Jimmy Delaney	Minneapolis	ND 10

1927

Jan 31	Chuck Wiggins	Cleveland	D 12
Feb 7	"Tiny" Jim Herman	Syracuse, NY	W 10
Feb 15	Tommy Loughran	Wilkes-Barre, PA	L 10
Feb 23	Jack DeMave	Grand Rapids, MI	D 10
Mar 8	Eddie Huffman	New York	KO 8
Mar 14	Chuck Wiggins	Indianapolis	ND 10
Mar 21	Sandy Siefert	Pittsburgh	W 10
Mar 28	Jimmy Slattery	Buffalo	LF 5
Apr 19	Quintin Romero Rojas	Wilkes-Barre, PA	W 10
May 9	Pat Lester	New York	W 10
May -	"Tiny" Jim Herman	Fremont, OH	ND 10
Jun 6	Joe Sekyra	Dayton, OH	ND 10
Jun 22	John "Chief" Metoquah	Indianapolis	ND 10
Jul 3	Sully Montgomery	Canton, OH	KO 3
Jul 13	Jack DeMave	Cleveland	W 10

Jul 21	Lou Scozza	Buffalo	W 10
Aug 25	Jack Gagnon	Boston	W 10
Aug 31	Joe Sekyra	Dayton, OH	W 12
Sep 14	Jack Delaney	Cleveland	W 10
Oct 13	Quintin Romero Rojas	Akron, OH	ND 10
Oct 26	Tom Heeney	Detroit	L 10
Nov 25	Paulino Uzcudun	New York	W 10
Dec 7	Phil Scott	Cleveland	W 10

1928

Mar 12	Jack Sharkey	New York	W 15
Jun 27	George Godfrey	New York	W 10
Jul 20	Johnny Squires	Detroit	W 10
Aug 15	Roberto Roberti	Brooklyn	LF 5
Sep 7	Ed "Bearcat" Wright	Omaha, NE	W 10
Nov -	Tut Jackson		W 10
Nov 30	Jim Maloney	Boston	L 10
Dec 28	Ernie Schaaf	Boston	L 10

1929

Jan 24	Tut Jackson	Jackson, MI	W 10
Feb 1	Max Schmeling	New York	LK 9
Apr 5	Otto von Porat	Boston	W 10
May 7	Emmett Rocco	Cleveland	L 12
Jun 17	George Cook	Boston	LF 5
Jun 27	Gerald "Tuffy" Griffith	Detroit	LF 7
Jul 29	Emmett Rocco	Cleveland	W 12
Sep 4	Meyer "K.O." Christner	Cleveland	LF 9
Oct 22	Jim Maloney	Cleveland	KO 2
Dec 9	Ernie Schaaf	Cleveland	W 12
Dec 27	Gerald "Tuffy" Griffith	New York	L 10

1930

Jan 20	Ricardo Bertazzolo	Cleveland	W 10
Feb 27	Vittorio Campolo	Miami	D 10
Mar 24	Vittorio Campolo	New York	W 10
Jun 19	Paulino Uzcudun	Detroit	W 10

Jul 2	Gerald "Tuffy" Griffith	Chicago	L 10
Sep 15	Babe Hunt	Oklahoma City	L 10
Oct 23	Dick Daniels	Boston	LF 4
Nov 7	Mickey Walker	Detroit	L 10
Dec 5	Jim Maloney	Boston	W 10

1931

Feb 6	Charley Retzlaff	Detroit	L 10
Feb 25	Mickey Walker	Miami	L 10
Mar 25	John Schwake	St. Louis	ND 10
Mar 30	Stanley Poreda	New York	L 10
Apr 6	Tom Heeney	Toronto	W 10
Apr 21	King Levinsky	Boston	W 10
May 5	Max Baer	Cleveland	W 10
Jul 3	Tony Galento	Cleveland	W 8
Aug 4	Meyer "K.O." Christner	Cleveland	W 12
Oct 19	Tommy Loughran	Philadelphia	L 10
Nov 9	Max Baer	San Francisco	L 10
Nov 20	Meyer "K.O." Christner	Cleveland	W 10

1932

Jun 24	Mickey Walker	Cleveland	W 12
Aug 1	Gerald "Tuffy" Griffith	Cleveland	W 12
Sep 1	King Levinsky	Cleveland	W 12

1933

Feb 24	King Levinsky	New York	W 10
Mar 28	Dick Daniels	Cleveland	L 10
Jun 20	Patsy Perroni	Cleveland	L 10
Jul 26	Tommy Loughran	Chicago	W 10
Oct 30	Big Boy Peterson	Houston	KO 6
Nov 9	Jack Van Noy	Dallas	L 10

1934

Jan 9	Jim Maloney	Miami	W 10
Mar 23	Bob Godwin	Daytona Beach	L 10
Jun 4	Natie Brown	Washington, DC	L 10

Jul 24	Patsy Perroni	Cleveland	L 10
Aug 1	Tommy Loughran	Freeport, NY	W 10
Aug 18	Adolph Wiater	Green Bay, WI	NC 3 *

May have been NC5 - bout halted by rain.

Dec 10	Patsy Perroni	Cleveland	L 10
Dec 18	Harry English	Toledo, OH	W 10
Dec 28	Charley Retzlaff	Minneapolis	L 10

1935

| Nov 11 | Jess Calhoun | Louisville | W 10 |

1936

Inactive

1937

Nov 17	Bob Olin	Cleveland	W 10
Dec 10	Jimmy Delaney	Lima, OH	KO 4
Dec 17 J	John Henry Lewis	Cleveland	L 10

1938

| Feb 3 | Georgie Brown | Cleveland | KO 3 |
| Feb 22 | Clarence "Red" Burman | Coral Gables | L 10 |

1939

Jul 26	Bob Sikes	Pine Bluff, AR	L 10
Aug 3	Young Allen	Macon, GA	L 10
Aug 14	Battling Blackjack	Tucson, AZ	KO 3
Aug 18	Babe Daniels	Phoenix	KO 4
Oct 2	Sandy Smith	Fort Smith, AR	W 10
Dec 14	Jack Lawton	Aiken, SC	KO 4

1940

| Jan 29 | Sandy McDonald | Hot Springs, AR | W 10 |
| Feb 19 | Tony Musto | Miami Beach | LK 3 |

Also by Jerry Fitch

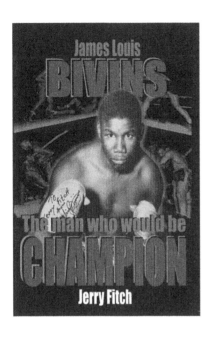

James Louis Bivins:
The Man Who Would Be Champion

ISBN 978-0-9543924-3-7

50 Years
of Fights, Fighters
and Friendships

ISBN 978-0-9543924-4-4

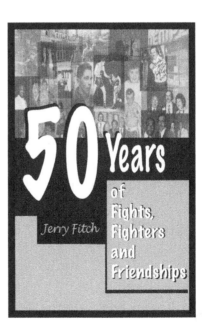

Also from Tora Books

The Gods of War
by
Springs Toledo

ISBN 978-0-9543924-5-1

Charley Burley
and
The Black Murderers' Row
by
Harry Otty

ISBN 978-0-9543924-2-0

Lightning Source UK Ltd.
Milton Keynes UK
UKOW06f1811100416

271973UK00006B/143/P